GLOBAL RESHAPING POLITICAL SHIFTS IN A POST-PANDEMIC WORLD

GLOBAL RESHAPING POLITICAL SHIFTS IN A POST-PANDEMIC WORLD

RAYAN MUSK

Mohammed Altaf Hussain

CONTENTS

Table of Content

Introduction

The beginning of the 21st century has been set apart by a progression of exceptional difficulties that have left a permanent engraving on the worldwide scene. The flare-up of the Coronavirus pandemic has made boundless obliteration general wellbeing as well as gone about as an impetus for a significant reshaping of political elements across the world. As countries wrestle with the diverse results of the pandemic, from monetary disturbances to social changes, the actual underpinnings of worldwide governmental issues are going through a seismic shift. In this complicated trap of progress, the shapes of force, strategy, and administration are being redrawn, proclaiming the approach of another period - a post-pandemic world that requests a reexamination of laid out standards and a recalibration of global relations.

The pandemic, in its persistent breadth across mainlands, has uncovered the weaknesses and interdependencies that tight spot countries together. As the infection rose above borders without any potential repercussions, it uncovered the insufficiencies of existing worldwide administration structures. The world wound up wrestling with a wellbeing emergency as well as with the results of a divided and clumsy reaction. The delicacy of the worldwide framework turned out to be incredibly obvious, provoking an aggregate reassessment of the requirement for more grounded worldwide coordinated effort. Despite an imperceptible foe, the basic for a planned and helpful methodology became undeniable, convincing countries to rise above international contentions and pool assets for everyone's benefit.

Besides, the pandemic has gone about as an impetus for thoughtfulness at the public level, provoking legislatures to reexamine their homegrown needs and strategies. The financial aftermath of lockdowns and disturbances has prodded a reconsideration of social wellbeing nets, medical services frameworks, and monetary designs. Legislatures are constrained to address the separation points that the emergency uncovered, with a developing accentuation on building strength and flexibility. This inner reconsideration, thusly, has expansive ramifications for the political scene, as pioneers are confronted with the basic to explore the fragile harmony between state power and individual opportunities.

In the monetary domain, the pandemic has set off a worldwide downturn of unmatched extent, causing an expanding influence that has reshaped the elements of global exchange and financial participation.

The disturbances to supply chains, the decrease in worldwide interest, and the speed increase of advanced change have adjusted the conventional forms of monetary power. Countries are constrained to reconsider their monetary procedures, with a reestablished center around independence, broadening, and the hug of arising innovations. The post-pandemic financial scene is portrayed by a shift towards a more multipolar world, where conventional monetary forces to be reckoned with are joined by arising players, and new roads for coordinated effort and rivalry arise.

Political changes in the post-pandemic world are not bound to the financial and medical care spaces; they stretch out into the domain of innovation and data. The speed increase of digitalization during lockdowns and remote work has changed the manner in which social orders capability as well as enhanced the job of innovation in political cycles. From contact following to the spread of data, innovation has turned into a necessary apparatus in the possession of legislatures, impacting the elements of observation, protection, and the activity of state power. As countries wrestle with the moral and administrative elements of mechanical headways, another outskirts of political contestation is arising, where the fight for impact reaches out into the internet and the domains of computerized reasoning and biotechnology.

The post-pandemic political scene is likewise described by a reconsideration of worldwide unions and organizations. The emergency has revealed the constraints of unilateralism and the requirement for cooperative ways to deal with address worldwide difficulties. Countries are recalibrating their conciliatory methodologies, looking for new coalitions, and building up existing organizations to explore the intricacies of a world in transition. Multilateral organizations, once addressed for their viability, are presently being revitalized as gatherings for aggregate activity and coordination. The international affairs of the post-pandemic time are set apart by a nuanced transaction of coalitions and competitions, with countries decisively situating themselves to get their inclinations in a quickly developing worldwide request.

Moreover, the social texture of countries is going through a significant change directly following the pandemic. The disturbances brought about by lockdowns, social removing measures, and financial difficulties have set off a reconsideration of cultural standards and values. Issues of imbalance, civil rights, and the job of the state in guaranteeing the government assistance of its residents have come to the very front. The pandemic has turned into an impetus for social developments and activism, intensifying voices that request fundamental change and a reconsidering of the common agreement. As social orders wrestle with the outcome of the emergency, the forms of political power are being molded by a more confident and informed populace, requesting responsibility and inclusivity from their states.

1. **Brief Overview of the Pandemic's Impact**

The coming of the Coronavirus pandemic in late 2019 introduced a worldwide emergency of unmatched extents, rising above borders and reshaping basically every feature of human life. As the infection spread with disturbing velocity, it brought to the front the delicacy of the interconnected world wherein we live. The quick and significant effect on general wellbeing was apparent as medical care frameworks all over the planet were extended as far as possible, wrestling with the flood in cases, deficiencies of clinical supplies, and the staggering loss of living souls. States were pushed into the unenviable place of going with quick and noteworthy choices, executing lockdowns, social separating measures, and travel limitations trying to check the spread of the infection. The once-unbelievable scenes of abandoned city roads and overpowered medical clinics turned into the distinct truth of a world in the pains of a pandemic.

Past the prompt wellbeing emergency, the financial aftermath of the pandemic resonated across the globe. The burden of lockdowns and limitations prompted disturbances in supply chains, the conclusion of organizations, and a flood of joblessness. The worldwide economy, when murmuring with movement, contracted at a disturbing rate, setting off a downturn of memorable extents. Private ventures confronted existential dangers, and weak populaces endured the worst part of monetary difficulties. Legislatures mixed to carry out boost bundles, financial measures, and social security nets to relieve the monetary effect, however the way to recuperation demonstrated long and difficult.

The pandemic's effect additionally reached out into the social texture of social orders. Social removing measures and lockdowns achieved significant changes in how individuals lived, worked, and associated. The sudden shift to remote work featured the computerized partition and highlighted the significance of innovation in keeping up with availability during seasons of segregation. School systems confronted uncommon difficulties as schools and colleges changed to web based picking up, fueling existing variations in admittance to training. In the interim, the pandemic uncovered and exacerbated social disparities, excessively influencing underestimated networks, bleeding edge laborers, and those with restricted admittance to medical services.

Amidst these difficulties, the pandemic exposed the qualities and shortcomings of administration structures around the world. The viability of a country's reaction turned into a basic measurement, for certain countries procuring acclaim for their quick and facilitated endeavors, while others confronted analysis for postponed reactions and deficient measures. The job of authority went under extraordinary examination, and the capacity of legislatures to impart successfully, ingrain certainty, and execute proof based strategies became vital. The emergency highlighted the significance of worldwide participation, as countries wrestled with the requirement for data sharing, joint examination endeavors, and cooperative immunization advancement.

Mainstream researchers assumed a focal part in the pandemic reaction, working energetically to figure out the infection, foster diagnostics, and eventually, make immunizations at an exceptional speed. The cooperative endeavors of scientists, drug organizations, and worldwide associations brought about the quick turn of events and dissemination of a few Coronavirus immunizations, offering a good omen in the battle against the infection. Be that as it may, the immunization roll-out likewise brought to the very front issues of antibody value, with abberations in access and conveyance reflecting more extensive worldwide imbalances.

The pandemic's effect on worldwide relations was significant, reconfiguring international scenes and modifying the elements of worldwide collaboration. The emergency provoked a reassessment of the job and viability of worldwide associations, like the World Wellbeing Association (WHO), and uncovered separation points in worldwide administration. The Unified Countries, previously confronting provokes in its capacity to resolve complex worldwide issues, wound up at the focal point of discussions over the ampleness of the global reaction. All the while, the pandemic exacerbated existing pressures between significant powers, featuring the international rivalry that endured even despite a common worldwide danger.

Additionally, the pandemic sped up previous patterns in innovation and development. As the world adjusted to remote work and computerized collaborations, the significance of innovation in day to day existence turned out to be more articulated. Internet business, telemedicine, and computerized correspondence stages experienced uncommon development, reshaping the business scene and speeding up the Fourth Modern Insurgency. Notwithstanding, the flood in dependence on computerized advances additionally raised worries about protection, network safety, and the potential for expanded observation.

In the domain of data and media, the pandemic powered an "infodemic" - a surge of deception and disinformation that spread as quickly as the actual infection. Paranoid fears, counterfeit fixes, and deluding data multiplied via online entertainment stages, representing a test to general wellbeing correspondence endeavors and adding to immunization reluctance. The pandemic highlighted the requirement for compelling science correspondence and media education to counter the unsafe impacts of deception.

As social orders wrestled with the significant and complex effect of the pandemic, a recharged center around strength, manageability, and worldwide collaboration arose. The emergency revealed the interconnectedness of the world and the requirement for aggregate activity to address prompt wellbeing dangers as well as more extensive difficulties, for example, environmental change, disparity, and the disintegration of popularity based standards. Requires a "green recuperation" got momentum, pushing for interests in practical and versatile frameworks that wouldn't just guide in that frame of mind from the pandemic yet in addition add to long haul ecological and social objectives.

2. The Catalyst for Political Transformation

The Coronavirus pandemic, an uncommon worldwide emergency, has shown to be an impetus for political change, setting off a reexamination of administration structures, global relations, and the actual underpinnings of cultural request. As countries wrestled with the complex difficulties presented by the infection, the pandemic uncovered weaknesses in existing political frameworks and prodded a flood of changes that rose above geological lines.

At the core of the political change was the reaction of state run administrations to the wellbeing emergency. The pandemic exposed the qualities and short-comings of various administration models, inciting a critical reassessment of state limit, authority viability, and the versatility of public foundations. Nations that had the option to mount quick, organized reactions with straightforward correspondence fared better in dealing with the wellbeing emergency, procuring the trust and certainty of their residents. On the other hand, those wrestling with postponed reactions, deficient assets, or political divisions confronted elevated investigation and public discontent.

In addition, the pandemic highlighted the sensitive harmony between state power and individual opportunities. As legislatures executed remarkable measures like lockdowns, observation advancements, and limitations on development to check the infection's spread, inquiries of common freedoms and the job of the state in the midst of emergency came to the front. The pressure between shielding general wellbeing and safeguarding individual freedoms turned into a focal subject in the political talk, with an enduring effect on the common agreement among residents and the state.

In the domain of worldwide relations, the pandemic went about as a pot, reshaping collusions, fueling existing international pressures, and rethinking the elements of worldwide collaboration. The emergency uncovered the restrictions of unilateralism and the basic for cooperative ways to deal with address shared difficulties. Global associations, remarkably the World Wellbeing Association (WHO), confronted examination and calls for change, featuring the requirement for a more successful and composed worldwide reaction instrument. The international relations of antibody dissemination further highlighted the transaction of force and obligation, as countries took part in immunization tact, displaying both fortitude and personal responsibility on the worldwide stage.

At the same time, the pandemic sped up patterns in deglobalization and patriotism. The disturbance of worldwide stockpile chains, travel limitations, and the basic for independence in basic areas provoked a reexamination of globalization's benefits. Nations tried to get their own advantages, focusing on homegrown worries over worldwide association. The strain between public interests and the interconnected idea of worldwide difficulties turned into a characterizing element of the pandemic's effect on global relations.

The monetary aftermath of the pandemic added one more layer to the political change, reshaping financial strategies, and complementing financial inconsistencies. States confronted the overwhelming undertaking of offsetting general wellbeing measures with the need to support financial movement. The organization of gigantic boost bundles, financial mediations, and social security nets became pivotal devices in exploring the monetary aftermath. Be that as it may, the lopsided dissemination of assets and the unique effect on various areas of society highlighted the requirement for additional comprehensive monetary strategies.

The pandemic-initiated monetary downturn featured the significance of flexibility and development. Businesses went through fast changes, for certain areas encountering phenomenal development, while others confronted existential dangers. The speed increase of digitalization, remote work, and internet business became meaningful of the advancing financial scene. The nexus among innovation and legislative issues turned out to be progressively articulated as legislatures wrestled with the difficulties and valuable open doors introduced by the advanced upset, including issues of information security, network safety, and the moral utilization of arising advances.

In the cultural circle, the pandemic went about as a mirror, reflecting and enhancing existing social imbalances and treacheries. Weak people group, including low-pay gatherings, minorities, and bleeding edge laborers, endured the worst part of the wellbeing and financial emergencies. The unbalanced effect revealed foundational disparities, filling social developments and calls for extraordinary change. Issues of racial equity, medical care access, and social security nets acquired noticeable quality, moving states to address profoundly instilled cultural variations.

The pandemic-instigated interruptions likewise prodded a reevaluation of cultural qualities and standards. The sudden shift to remote work and computerized connections provoked reflections on balance between serious and fun activities, the idea of fundamental work, and the worth of local area. Emotional wellness contemplations moved to the very front as people wrestled with detachment, vulnerability, and the drawn out ramifications of the emergency. The versatility of networks and the rise of grassroots drives highlighted the job of common society in molding the political account and upholding for social change.

Moreover, the pandemic filled in as a litmus test for the strength of popularity based organizations. Nations with powerful equitable practices confronted difficulties in offsetting general wellbeing goals with majority rule standards. Crisis powers, limitations on get together, and the utilization of innovation for observation raised worries about the disintegration of vote based standards. The sensitive dance between emergency the executives and the protection of popularity based values turned into a focal subject, with suggestions for the eventual fate of majority rule administration in a world wrestling with perplexing and interconnected difficulties.

3. **Purpose and Scope of the Book**

This book plans to investigate the complex effect of arising innovations on society, analyzing how mechanical progressions shape our lives, impact dynamic cycles, and reclassify the actual texture of our interconnected world. In a period set apart by quick advancement, this investigation digs into the extraordinary force of advances like man-made reasoning, biotechnology, and blockchain, planning to disentangle their suggestions across different areas.

The motivation behind this try is to give a nuanced comprehension of the intricate interchange among innovation and society. It looks to rise above oversimplified accounts and address the significant inquiries emerging from the coordination of innovation into the center of human life. Instead of introducing a deterministic perspective on innovative advancement, the book explores the complex territory of moral problems, cultural changes, and the developing connection among people and the advances that encompass them.

The extent of this book stretches out across different elements of contemporary life. It looks at the effect of arising advances on the economy, instruction, medical services, and administration. By winding around together experiences from different disciplines, the aim is to offer perusers a far reaching point of view on the more extensive ramifications of innovative progressions. From the moral contemplations of hereditary designing to the cultural outcomes of algorithmic direction, every part adds to a comprehensive comprehension of the unpredictable embroidery that innovation winds inside the structure holding the system together.

In addition, the book doesn't avoid tending to the possible dangers and difficulties presented by mechanical headways. It basically evaluates issues, for example, protection concerns, network safety dangers, and the computerized partition, recognizing that the commitments of development come inseparably with liabilities. By drawing in with the more obscure features of mechanical advancement, this investigation tries to enable perusers with the information and mindfulness important to explore the intricacies of a tech-driven world.

In the journey to disentangle the effect of arising advancements, the book takes on an interdisciplinary methodology. It draws on experiences from fields as different as software engineering, morals, humanism, financial matters, and political theory. This interdisciplinary focal point considers a more all encompassing assessment of the perplexing connections among innovation and society. It empowers the investigation of the specialized parts of advancement as well as the socio-social, moral, and political aspects that shape and are formed by innovation.

All through the story, the book endeavors to figure out some kind of harmony among openness and profundity. Perceiving the different foundations of its readership, it distils complex ideas into edible experiences without settling on the scholarly meticulousness expected for a careful comprehension. Whether one is knowledgeable in innovation or moving toward the subject interestingly, the book means to be a significant asset, offering an entryway to investigate the many-sided scene of arising advances and their effect on the world we possess.

Chapter 1

The Pandemic's Wake

The wake of the Coronavirus pandemic reaches out a long ways past the quick well-being emergency, making swells that touch each part of our worldwide society. As the world wrestles with the result of this phenomenal occasion, the significant effect on general wellbeing, economies, social orders, and administration structures turns out to be progressively clear.

The most quick and instinctive result of the pandemic is the cost it has taken on general wellbeing. The infection has asserted large number of lives around the world, uncovering weaknesses in medical care frameworks and exposing the disparities that exist in admittance to clinical consideration. Overpowered clinics, deficiencies of clinical supplies, and the sheer size of the emergency have incited an aggregate retribution with the condition of worldwide medical services foundation. The pandemic has uncovered the delicacy of general wellbeing frameworks and the requirement for key interests in readiness, exploration, and worldwide joint effort to address the ongoing emergency as well as future wellbeing dangers.

Past the stunning death toll, the pandemic has fashioned monetary ruin on a worldwide scale. Lockdowns, travel limitations, and interruptions to supply binds have prompted a serious constriction of economies, driving numerous nations into downturn. Private ventures, the foundation of numerous economies, confronted terminations, and joblessness rates took off.

Legislatures answered with extraordinary boost bundles, endeavoring to settle economies and forestall broad monetary difficulty. In any case, the monetary aftermath has been lopsided, compounding existing imbalances and leaving weak populaces especially defenseless to the financial slump.

The pandemic-prompted monetary downturn has likewise featured the interconnectedness of worldwide business sectors. The disturbances in a single region of the planet resound across borders, influencing supply chains, exchange, and venture. The requirement for versatility and enhancement in monetary designs has turned into a squeezing worry, with countries reconsidering their reliance on specific businesses and worldwide organizations. The post-pandemic financial scene is one of recalibration, where versatility and development are principal for recuperation and supported development.

Cultural changes right after the pandemic are similarly significant. The unexpected shift to remote work and online instruction has sped up computerized change, changing the manner in which individuals live, work, and learn. This change in perspective has extensive ramifications for the eventual fate of work, metropolitan preparation, and the idea of human associations. The computerized partition, when a stewing issue, has become extremely obvious as differences in admittance to innovation and the web have enlarged, extending existing imbalances.

The pandemic has likewise ignited a reexamination of cultural qualities and needs. The aggregate insight of living through a worldwide emergency has incited reflection on the importance of local area, fortitude, and strength. As people wrestle with confinement, vulnerability, and misfortune, there is a developing consciousness of the significance of emotional well-being and prosperity. The job of social designs, encouraging groups of people, and local area commitment in cultivating versatility has come to the very front, moving social orders to focus on comprehensive ways to deal with wellbeing and satisfaction.

Besides, the pandemic has gone about as an impetus for social developments and activism. Issues of racial unfairness, financial imbalance, and fundamental blemishes in administration stand out. The interconnection of emergencies has enlightened the differences that exist inside social orders, inciting requests for fundamental change. Grassroots developments upholding for civil rights, natural manageability, and impartial admittance to assets have picked up speed, flagging a developing familiarity with the requirement for an additional equitable and comprehensive world.

In the domain of administration, the pandemic has tried the adequacy of political authority and the heartiness of majority rule organizations. Pioneers confronted the test of offsetting general wellbeing objectives with common freedoms, exploring the almost negligible difference between implementing limitations and safeguarding individual opportunities.

Crisis powers, information protection concerns, and the job of innovation in reconnaissance have become petulant issues, featuring the sensitive harmony between emergency the executives and maintaining popularity based standards.

The worldwide reaction to the pandemic has likewise highlighted the significance of global participation and the job of multilateral establishments. The World Wellbeing Association (WHO) confronted both honor and analysis for its treatment of the emergency, igniting banters about the requirement for change in worldwide wellbeing administration. The immunization rollout, set apart by differences in dispersion and access, has additionally underscored the need of a planned worldwide reaction to address the prompt wellbeing emergency as well as the drawn out difficulties presented by irresistible illnesses.

The pandemic's wake has sped up previous patterns in innovation and advancement. The computerized speed increase saw during lockdowns has moved progressions in regions like man-made brainpower, telemedicine, and far off joint effort. The job of innovation in molding the post-pandemic world is huge, impacting the way in which social orders capability, how state run administrations convey administrations, and how organizations work. The moral components of innovation use, including issues of protection, security, and the evenhanded dispersion of advantages, have become vital to conversations about the future direction of development.

Right after the pandemic, natural contemplations have likewise acquired noticeable quality. The brief stoppage in human action during lockdowns offered a brief look at diminished discharges and ecological recovery. This has prodded discussions about supportable turn of events, the effect of human action in the world, and the dire requirement for aggregate activity to address environmental change. The pandemic has filled in as a reminder, stressing the interconnectedness of human and natural wellbeing and the basic to construct an additional practical and versatile future.

As social orders explore the complicated territory of recuperation and reproduction, the examples gained from the pandemic become fundamental guideposts for what's in store. The basic isn't just to reconstruct what has been disturbed yet to reconsider frameworks and designs in manners that encourage inclusivity, value, and maintainability. The pandemic's wake fills in as a pot, producing an aggregate comprehension of the weaknesses uncovered and the open doors for positive change. It is a source of inspiration, encouraging people, networks, and countries to gain from the emergency and work cooperatively towards a stronger, just, and interconnected world.

1.1 Global Health Crisis and its Ramifications

The worldwide wellbeing emergency released by the Coronavirus pandemic has resounded across each aspect of human life, making a permanent imprint on social orders, economies, and administration structures around the world. Past the quick danger to general wellbeing, the pandemic has gotten under way an outpouring of repercussions, revealing weaknesses and provoking a crucial reconsideration of readiness, flexibility, and worldwide participation.

At the focal point of this emergency is the significant effect on general wellbeing. The infection, novel and profoundly infectious, took advantage of the interconnectedness of our globalized world, rising above borders with disturbing velocity. Wellbeing frameworks in numerous countries ended up extended as far as possible, wrestling with the flood in cases, deficiencies of clinical supplies, and the staggering interest for basic consideration. The stunning loss of living souls has not exclusively been a serious demonstration of the seriousness of the wellbeing emergency yet has likewise highlighted the desperation of invigorating worldwide wellbeing framework.

The repercussions of the wellbeing emergency reach out past the quick cost for life. Long stretch results are surfacing as survivors wrestle with waiting medical problems, generally alluded to as "long Coronavirus." The acknowledgment of these tireless wellbeing provokes adds one more layer of intricacy to the post-pandemic scene, requesting a complete comprehension of the infection's effect on both intense and constant wellbeing results.

Moreover, the pandemic has exposed the current separation points in medical care availability and value. Variations in medical care access, both inside and between nations, have been distinctly enlightened. Weak people group, frequently with restricted admittance to quality medical care, have borne the brunt of the emergency. The significance of tending to these differences in wellbeing results has turned into a focal subject in the worldwide talk on general wellbeing, featuring the requirement for comprehensive and fair wellbeing frameworks.

The financial aftermath originating from the worldwide wellbeing emergency is similarly critical. The inconvenience of lockdowns, travel limitations, and social separating measures pointed toward checking the infection's spread hastened a financial downturn of uncommon scale. Organizations covered, supply chains were upset, and millions confronted joblessness as financial movement came to a standstill. The flexibility of economies was tried, and the requirement for versatile monetary techniques turned out to be completely clear.

States answered with monstrous monetary improvement bundles, intending to fight off the most exceedingly terrible financial effects and give a security net to people and organizations.

In any case, the monetary recuperation has been lopsided, with areas like the travel industry, cordiality, and private companies confronting delayed difficulties. The worldwide idea of the monetary slump underlined the reliance of countries in a firmly associated world, complementing the significance of global participation in tending to financial difficulties.

Additionally, the monetary repercussions of the wellbeing emergency have exacerbated existing imbalances. Financial differences have augmented as minimized networks, frequently lopsidedly impacted by the infection, face more noteworthy monetary difficulties. The "K-molded" recuperation, where certain areas experience fast bounce back while others mull, has highlighted the split between the wealthy and the poor. The test ahead isn't just to remake economies however to do as such that locations and redresses these glaring imbalances.

Cultural changes put into high gear by the pandemic have been significant, modifying the manner in which individuals live, work, and connect. The unexpected shift to remote work and online schooling, driven by lockdowns and social separating measures, has sped up computerized change. The ramifications are huge, going from the reconfiguration of metropolitan spaces and driving examples to the advancement of work culture and the idea of social connections.

This change, while cultivating network in a period of actual confinement, has likewise revealed the computerized partition. Differences in admittance to innovation and the web have become obstructions to schooling, business, and medical services, compounding existing disparities. Connecting this computerized hole has turned into a need in guaranteeing that the advantages of the advanced age are open to all, as opposed to additionally packing potential open doors in the possession of the carefully special.

The pandemic has incited a reexamination of cultural qualities and needs. As people group wrestle with vulnerability, misfortune, and disconnection, there is a developing acknowledgment of the significance of psychological wellness and prosperity. The attention on comprehensive wellbeing, enveloping mental, profound, and social aspects, has acquired unmistakable quality. The meaning of local area strength and encouraging groups of people in exploring emergencies has become evident, underscoring the interconnectedness of individual and cultural prosperity.

Furthermore, the wellbeing emergency has filled in as an impetus for social developments and activism, pointing out previous cultural issues. The crossing difficulties of the pandemic, monetary downturn, and calls for racial equity have touched off developments upholding for fundamental change. The interest for impartial admittance to assets, civil rights, and ecological maintainability has picked up speed, pushing social orders to stand up to profoundly imbued disparities and address them at their foundations.

Administration structures have confronted uncommon difficulties during the worldwide wellbeing emergency. The viability of political authority in exploring the intricacies of the pandemic has been examined. Pioneers have wrestled with the sensitive harmony between protecting general wellbeing and saving individual opportunities, frequently confronting analysis for either overextend or inadequate measures. The emergency has highlighted the significance of straightforward correspondence, proof based navigation, and the requirement for vigorous emergency the executives capacities in administration.

The worldwide reaction to the wellbeing emergency plays highlighted the part of global collaboration and the viability of multilateral foundations. The World Wellbeing Association (WHO), specifically, ended up at the focal point of discussions over its ability and authority in dealing with a worldwide wellbeing crisis. The requirement for cooperative endeavors in research, asset sharing, and antibody dispersion has underscored the interconnectedness of the worldwide local area in tending to wellbeing challenges.

The immunization rollout, a critical stage in the worldwide wellbeing emergency reaction, has uncovered the two victories and difficulties. The phenomenal speed of antibody improvement and circulation grandstands the abilities of logical development and worldwide coordinated effort. Notwithstanding, issues of immunization value, appropriation planned operations, and antibody aversion have raised moral and down to earth difficulties. The fair circulation of immunizations worldwide remaining parts a basic part of the post-pandemic recuperation, highlighting the significance of fortitude and aggregate activity in defeating shared difficulties.

Mechanical progressions play had a urgent impact in answering the wellbeing emergency. From the improvement of immunizations at an exceptional speed to the utilization of computerized apparatuses for contact following and checking, innovation has demonstrated instrumental in different parts of pandemic administration. Notwithstanding, this dependence on innovation has likewise brought about moral worries, especially in regards to protection, reconnaissance, and the expected abuse of information. Adjusting the advantages of mechanical development with moral contemplations is a basic part of exploring the advancing scene formed by the worldwide wellbeing emergency.

Natural contemplations have likewise been pushed into the spotlight during the pandemic. The impermanent decrease in human action during lockdowns prompted a perceptible diminishing in contamination and a break for the climate. This potentially negative result has provoked conversations about the connection between human exercises, natural corruption, and the basic for reasonable practices. The pandemic has elevated mindfulness about the interconnectedness of human and natural wellbeing, underlining the earnestness of taking on strategies and ways of behaving that advance supportability.

1.2 Economic Fallout and Social Disruptions

The financial aftermath and social interruptions set off by the Coronavirus pandemic have spread out a significant and sweeping effect, reshaping the texture of social orders and economies all over the planet. The exceptional idea of the emergency has exposed weaknesses in existing designs, provoking a reconsideration of financial standards, cultural standards, and the actual groundworks of administration.

At the center of the pandemic's repercussions is the seismic shock to worldwide economies. The burden of lockdowns, travel limitations, and social separating measures to contain the infection's spread accelerated a monetary slump of unrivaled extents. Organizations confronted terminations, supply chains were disturbed, and joblessness rates took off, prompting a worldwide downturn that unfurled with extraordinary speed. The versatility of economies was tried as they wrestled with the twin difficulties of protecting general wellbeing and relieving the monetary aftermath.

Legislatures, perceiving the direness of mediation, answered with monstrous financial improvement bundles, money related measures, and social security nets. These endeavors meant to settle economies, forestall far reaching monetary difficulty, and backing organizations and people through the wild period. Nonetheless, the financial effect has been lopsided, fueling existing imbalances and uncovering abberations in the capacity of countries to face the hardship. The post-pandemic financial scene is set apart by the basic to modify with strength, address primary shortcomings, and establish the groundwork for maintainable and comprehensive development.

The pandemic-actuated monetary slump has highlighted the interconnectedness of worldwide business sectors. Disturbances in a single region of the planet have resonated across borders, influencing exchange, venture, and supply chains. The dependence on worldwide joint effort for financial dependability has become clear, underlining the requirement for helpful techniques and the significance of an organized worldwide reaction to shared monetary difficulties.

Moreover, the pandemic has complemented existing financial differences. Weak populaces, including low-pay gatherings, casual laborers, and underestimated networks, have borne the brunt of the financial difficulties. The "K-formed" recuperation, where certain areas experience fast bounce back while others grieve, has extended the hole between the favored and the distraught. As social orders wrestle with the monetary aftermath, there is a developing acknowledgment of the requirement for comprehensive financial strategies that address fundamental imbalances and guarantee that the recuperation helps all portions of society.

The change of work and the work environment has been one of the characterizing social interruptions set off by the pandemic. The unexpected shift to remote work, driven by lockdowns and social separating measures, has sped up computerized change and adjusted the elements of business. While remote work has empowered business congruity, it has likewise uncovered the computerized partition, as not every person has had equivalent admittance to the vital innovation and web framework. The hybridization of work models, consolidating remote and in-person components, has turned into a point of convergence in conversations about the eventual fate of work and its suggestions for efficiency, representative prosperity, and hierarchical designs.

Likewise, the training area has gone through a change in perspective, with schools and colleges adjusting to web based learning models. The computerized partition in training has turned into a major problem, with variations in admittance to innovation and the web fueling instructive imbalances. The difficulties of remote picking up, including issues of commitment, computerized proficiency, and the social parts of schooling, have provoked a reexamination of school systems and the requirement for imaginative ways to deal with guarantee kept learning in an advanced age.

The pandemic has additionally influenced the elements of urbanization and city arranging. The conventional models of thickly populated metropolitan habitats have been addressed as the pandemic featured weaknesses in packed day to day environments. Remote work, combined with the expanded accentuation on wellbeing and prosperity, has incited conversations about the potential de-densification of metropolitan regions and the reconsidering of metropolitan intending to make stronger, economical, and bearable urban communities.

Cultural qualities and standards have gone through critical changes in light of the pandemic. The aggregate insight of living through a worldwide emergency has incited reflection on the significance of local area, fortitude, and individual prosperity. Emotional well-being contemplations have acquired conspicuousness as people wrestle with detachment, vulnerability, and the mental cost of the emergency. The pandemic has started discussions about the idea of bliss, the job of work in our lives, and the significance of social associations, reshaping cultural needs and testing customary thoughts of accomplishment and satisfaction.

Besides, the wellbeing emergency has gone about as an impetus for social developments and activism. Issues of racial unfairness, financial disparity, and foundational blemishes in administration certainly stand out. The pandemic has enlightened and intensified existing variations inside social orders, inciting calls for foundational change. Grassroots developments supporting for civil rights, ecological maintainability, and impartial admittance to assets have picked up speed, flagging a developing familiarity with the requirement for an additional equitable and comprehensive world.

The emergency has highlighted the significance of social security nets and the job of state run administrations in guaranteeing the prosperity of their residents. The insufficiencies of existing social emotionally supportive networks have been revealed, prompting conversations about the requirement for far reaching government assistance strategies, general medical services, and measures to address pay disparity. The cultural reaction to the pandemic has revived banters about the common agreement, individual privileges, and the obligations of legislatures in the midst of emergency.

In the domain of administration, the pandemic has tried the viability of political authority and the strength of vote based foundations. Pioneers have confronted the test of offsetting general wellbeing goals with common freedoms, exploring the barely recognizable difference between authorizing limitations and protecting individual opportunities. Crisis powers, information security concerns, and the job of innovation in observation have become hostile issues, featuring the fragile harmony between emergency the executives and maintaining vote based standards.

The worldwide reaction to the wellbeing emergency plays highlighted the part of global collaboration and the adequacy of multilateral foundations. The World Wellbeing Association (WHO) has wound up at the focal point of discussions over its ability and authority in dealing with a worldwide wellbeing crisis. The requirement for cooperative endeavors in research, asset sharing, and immunization appropriation has underscored the interconnectedness of the worldwide local area in tending to wellbeing challenges.

As the world explores the mind boggling landscape of recuperation and recreation, the illustrations gained from the monetary aftermath and social interruptions created by the pandemic become fundamental guideposts for what's to come. The basic isn't just to modify what has been disturbed yet to do as such that locations and redresses glaring imbalances, encourages flexibility, and establishes the groundwork for a more comprehensive, supportable, and evenhanded world. The post-pandemic period requires an aggregate rethinking of cultural designs, monetary frameworks, and administration systems to address the difficulties of a quickly developing worldwide scene.

1.3 Initial Political Responses

The flare-up of the Coronavirus pandemic set off a worldwide emergency that requested quick and definitive political reactions from states all over the planet. The underlying political reactions to the pandemic were set apart by an intricate exchange of general wellbeing objectives, monetary contemplations, and the need to explore extraordinary difficulties. This multi-layered emergency uncovered weaknesses in administration structures, tried the viability of political authority, and highlighted the basic for composed global endeavors.

At the beginning of the pandemic, the essential focal point of political reactions was on general wellbeing measures pointed toward containing the spread of the infection. Legislatures carried out a scope of procedures, including lockdowns, social separating measures, travel limitations, and far reaching testing. The seriousness of the wellbeing emergency required a quick and frequently radical preparation of assets, featuring the focal job of political dynamic in molding the direction of the pandemic.

The viability of these general wellbeing measures changed broadly, reflecting contrasts in administration designs, assets, and political will. Nations that had the option to execute early and rigid measures, combined with clear and straightforward correspondence, frequently fared better in controlling the spread of the infection. Conversely, postponed reactions, conflicting informing, and difficulties in carrying out general wellbeing measures added to the heightening of cases in certain districts.

The pandemic additionally exposed the qualities and shortcomings of medical care frameworks all around the world. Countries with hearty and well-resourced medical care frameworks were better prepared to deal with the flood in cases, giving opportune clinical consideration and keeping a more powerful reaction. On the other hand, nations with stressed medical services frameworks confronted huge difficulties, wrestling with deficiencies of clinical supplies, overpowered medical clinics, and an absence of basic consideration assets. The differences in medical care limit turned into a point of convergence of political conversations, provoking calls for expanded interests in medical services foundation and a reexamination of worldwide wellbeing needs.

The pandemic's crossing point with political philosophies and administration styles became apparent in the variety of reactions. Dictator systems frequently forced severe measures with an emphasis on brought together control, while popular governments confronted the sensitive errand of offsetting general wellbeing goals with individual opportunities. The pressure between the requirement for unequivocal activity and the protection of common freedoms turned into a repetitive topic, provoking discussions about the fitting job of the state in the midst of emergency.

The financial aftermath of the pandemic incited states to execute phenomenal monetary measures to alleviate the effect on organizations and people. Improvement bundles, monetary guide, and social wellbeing nets were sent to forestall boundless financial difficulty and settle economies. The scale and nature of monetary mediations shifted, reflecting both the seriousness of the financial slump and the financial limit of individual countries.

The political reactions to the monetary difficulties were portrayed by a fragile difficult exercise. States confronted the double basic of defending general wellbeing through lockdowns and limitations while at the same time tending to the monetary outcomes of these actions.

The monetary aftermath lopsidedly impacted specific areas, like accommodation, the travel industry, and private companies, provoking designated mediations to forestall far and wide insolvencies and employment misfortunes.

The worldwide interconnectedness of economies turned into a focal subject in political reactions to the financial emergency. The disturbances in worldwide stock chains, exchange, and travel highlighted the requirement for global collaboration to address shared financial difficulties. Calls for fortitude and cooperation acquired unmistakable quality as countries perceived the impediments of one-sided approaches despite a worldwide monetary slump.

Besides, the pandemic's financial effect exacerbated existing imbalances inside social orders. Weak populaces, including low-pay gatherings, casual specialists, and under-estimated networks, confronted uplifted monetary difficulties. The variations in admittance to assets, instructive open doors, and social emotionally supportive net-works turned out to be extremely clear, provoking political conversations about the requirement for comprehensive and fair financial approaches.

Notwithstanding general wellbeing and financial contemplations, political reactions additionally wrestled with the cultural interruptions set off by the pandemic. The sudden shift to remote work and online instruction incited a reconsideration of cul-tural standards, work structures, and the computerized partition. States explored the difficulties of adjusting to new methods of work and instruction while resolving issues of access, advanced education, and the social components of far off cooperations.

The pandemic's effect on emotional well-being arisen as a huge cultural concern. Confinement, vulnerability, and the mental cost of the emergency incited political conversations about the significance of mental prosperity and the requirement for vigorous psychological wellness emotionally supportive networks. The crossing point of the wellbeing emergency with more extensive cultural issues, including racial foul play, featured the interconnected idea of social difficulties and incited political reac-tions that recognized and tended to foundational disparities.

Political reactions were not restricted to individual countries; the pandemic incited a reassessment of the job and viability of global associations. The World Wellbeing As-sociation (WHO) ended up at the focal point of discussions over its ability to facilitate a worldwide reaction and its reliance on part states for financing and collaboration. The difficulties looked by worldwide organizations in exploring international strains, guaranteeing fair immunization circulation, and tending to worldwide wellbeing variations highlighted the intricacies of worldwide administration notwithstanding a common emergency.

The turn of events and dispersion of immunizations turned into a point of convergence of political reactions as the pandemic advanced.

State run administrations participated in immunization tact, acquirement ex-changes, and endeavors to guarantee far reaching antibody access. The lopsided circu-lation of immunizations and issues of antibody value featured the moral and political difficulties innate in dealing with a worldwide public great during an emergency. The pandemic highlighted the requirement for worldwide cooperation in exploration, improvement, and dissemination of clinical mediations, underscoring the intercon-nectedness of worldwide wellbeing.

Mechanical progressions assumed a vital part in political reactions to the pandemic. Computerized instruments for contact following, checking, and correspondence became necessary to general wellbeing methodologies. The utilization of innovation in remote work, telemedicine, and antibody dispersion displayed the potential for development to address difficulties presented by the emergency. Notwithstanding, the expanded dependence on innovation additionally raised moral worries, including issues of protection, observation, and the computerized partition, provoking political conversations about the capable utilization of innovation in emergency the executives.

Chapter 2

Redefining Nationalism

The idea of patriotism, when considered a generally steady and distinct political philosophy, has gone through huge changes as of late. The moving elements of worldwide governmental issues, financial relationship, and social trades have provoked a reconsideration and, at times, a redefinition of patriotism. This developing peculiarity is described by an intricate exchange of personality, sway, and worldwide interconnectedness, testing customary ideas and reshaping the manner in which countries see and express their aggregate characters.

Patriotism, at its center, is frequently connected with a feeling of shared personality, culture, history, and an aggregate feeling of having a place inside a particular topographical space. By and large, patriotism has been a strong power in molding political developments, driving decolonization, and rousing freedom battles. Notwithstanding, the contemporary scene presents new layers of intricacy, provoking countries to explore the strains between public pride, worldwide collaboration, and the real factors of an interconnected world.

One part of the advancing patriot talk is the pressure among patriotism and globalism. While patriotism customarily stresses the significance of public sway, lines, and independence, the rising interconnectedness of the globalized world difficulties these goals.

Financial reliance, worldwide organizations, and shared worldwide difficulties, for example, environmental change and pandemics, expect countries to team up and explore complex global organizations. This has led to a nuanced type of patriotism that looks to offset public interests with the acknowledgment of shared worldwide obligations.

In the financial domain, the customary story of monetary patriotism, set apart by protectionist strategies and an emphasis on homegrown ventures, is being rethought. Worldwide stockpile chains, economic alliance, and global monetary participation have obscured the lines between simply public and global interests. Countries progressively end up enmeshed in a sensitive dance, looking to safeguard homegrown businesses while recognizing the advantages of worldwide exchange and monetary coordinated effort. This financial patriotism is portrayed by a down to earth approach that tries to offset public interests with the real factors of a globalized economy.

Besides, the ascent of egalitarian developments in different regions of the planet has added to a redefinition of patriotism. Egalitarian pioneers frequently benefit from patriot opinions, accentuating the assurance of public character, culture, and values. In any case, this brand of patriotism can once in a while appear in exclusionary works on, filling xenophobia and nativism. The pressure between a more comprehensive type of urban patriotism and an exclusionary ethno-patriotism becomes clear as countries wrestle with issues of migration, social variety, and the meaning of who has a place with the country.

The topic of character inside the patriot talk is multi-layered. The ascent of personality governmental issues, energized by issues of identity, religion, and social legacy, meets with patriot stories. Countries wrestle with the test of encouraging a firm public character that obliges different networks inside their nation. The redefinition of patriotism includes exploring the harmony between a bringing together public story and the acknowledgment of numerous characters that add to the rich embroidery of a country.

In the domain of innovation, the computerized age has worked with new types of patriotism and transnationalism. Virtual entertainment, specifically, assumes a critical part in forming and enhancing patriot stories. Online stages can act as discussions for the scattering of nationalistic feelings, yet they additionally rise above borders, permitting people to interface, share thoughts, and structure transnational networks in view of shared interests or personalities. The crossing point of innovation and patriotism brings up issues about the effect of virtual spaces on the development of public characters and the potential for both solidarity and division in the web-based domain.

Natural worries have additionally become interwoven with the patriot talk. Shared difficulties, for example, environmental change, deforestation, and biodiversity misfortune require global collaboration, testing the conventional accentuation on one-sided public interests.

The redefinition of patriotism in this setting includes perceiving the interconnectedness of biological frameworks and the requirement for cooperative endeavors to address worldwide natural emergencies.

The Coronavirus pandemic has additionally confounded the connection among patriotism and worldwide participation. While the underlying reaction to the pandemic accentuated public measures, for example, line terminations and homegrown lockdowns, the resulting eases highlighted the need of worldwide cooperation in regions like antibody dispersion, information sharing, and exploration. The pandemic uncovered the restrictions of simply nationalistic methodologies in tending to worldwide wellbeing emergencies, stressing the requirement for a more helpful and facilitated reaction.

The redefinition of patriotism is additionally apparent in the advancing job of worldwide establishments. While a few patriot developments advocate for a decrease in the impact of supranational substances, others perceive the significance of these organizations in tending to worldwide difficulties. The unease among patriotism and internationalism is overwhelming in banters about the job of associations like the Unified Countries, the European Association, and the World Wellbeing Association. Countries are recalibrating their commitment with these foundations, trying to attest their power while recognizing the advantages of multilateral cooperation.

In the social space, the redefinition of patriotism includes a reassessment of social legacy, articulation, and impact. Countries wrestle with the pressure between safeguarding conventional social characters and drawing in with worldwide social streams. The spread of data, thoughts, and mainstream society across borders difficulties the idea of a homogeneous public culture. This prompts countries to rethink their way to deal with social variety, perceiving the worth of worldwide impacts while safeguarding one of a kind social articulations.

The re-imagined patriotism likewise crosses with issues of basic liberties and civil rights. Developments upholding for correspondence, equity, and the privileges of minimized networks challenge patriot stories that propagate fundamental disparities. The pressure between a patriotism established in selectiveness and one that embraces inclusivity turns into a point of convergence in political talk. Countries are progressively constrained to address authentic treacheries, advance social attachment, and guarantee that patriot feelings line up with standards of common freedoms and fairness.

2.1 The Surge of Nationalistic Sentiments

The flood of nationalistic opinions lately has denoted a prominent change in the worldwide political scene, with countries all over the planet seeing a resurgence of intense positive energy and personality driven governmental issues. This rise in patriotism is a complicated and complex peculiarity, impacted by a conjunction of variables, for example, monetary vulnerabilities, migration challenges, social nerves, and the more extensive effects of globalization. As countries wrestle with these elements, the flood of nationalistic feelings is reshaping political talk, approaches, and the actual idea of worldwide communications.

Financial variables assume a vital part in energizing the ascent of nationalistic feelings. Times of financial vulnerability and stagnation frequently make rich ground for patriot developments to flourish. The commitment of financial restoration and the insurance of homegrown enterprises become focal fundamentals of patriot plans, reverberating with sections of the populace who feel abandoned by globalization. The apparent danger to occupations, monetary security, and the general prosperity of residents turns into an energizing point for patriot pioneers, outlining their story as far as protecting public interests against apparent outside dangers.

Movement, one more huge impetus for the flood of nationalistic opinions, interweaves with financial worries to enhance patriot manner of speaking. The apprehension about losing positions to migrants, social conflicts, and tensions about public character become central focuses for patriot developments. Pioneers who tap into these worries frequently utilize a manner of speaking of protectionism and boundary security, promising to safeguard their countries from the apparent adverse consequences of migration. This account encourages an "us against them" attitude, underlining the need to focus on the interests of the local populace over those of seen pariahs.

Social nerves likewise add to the ascent of nationalistic opinions. As social orders become more different because of relocation, globalization, and expanded network, a few people might feel a feeling of social removal or misfortune. Patriot developments frequently exploit these nerves, promising to safeguard and reestablish an apparent conventional public character. The accentuation on social homogeneity and a re-visitation of a nostalgic vision of the past reverberates with the people who feel a feeling of disquiet notwithstanding fast social changes.

The flood of nationalistic feelings is additionally intently attached to inquiries of power and independence. In a time of worldwide relationship and global organiza-tions, patriot developments frequently lift up recovering public power.

The pushback against saw outside impact or impedance reverberates with the indi-viduals who feel that their country's independence is dissolving. Issues like economic deals, worldwide associations, and unions become landmarks for patriots looking to state their countries' autonomy and focus on homegrown direction.

Virtual entertainment and innovation assume a crucial part in enhancing and spreading nationalistic opinions. Online stages give a space to the fast spread of patriot stories, empowering developments to universally interface with similar people. On-line entertainment can make closed quarters where patriot thoughts are supported, encouraging a feeling of local area among the individuals who share comparative opin-ions. The speed and reach of advanced correspondence add to the quick assembly of patriot developments, permitting them to rise above geological limits and construct transnational organizations.

The flood of nationalistic opinions is much of the time joined by a dismissal of globalism, described by distrust toward worldwide participation and global estab-lishments. Patriot developments might see worldwide administration structures as infringements on public power and stages that don't satisfactorily address their inclinations. This dismissal of globalism can appear in requires the renegotiation of peaceful accords, the withdrawal from specific associations, and the advancement of a decisive, confident public personality.

Verifiable stories and aggregate memory assume a huge part in molding the flood of nationalistic feelings. Patriot developments regularly draw on verifiable occasions, genuine or saw, to build a story that supports a feeling of public personality and pride. This particular utilization of history frequently features snapshots of seen public mag-nificence while making light of or precluding less positive viewpoints. By outlining verifiable occasions through a patriot focal point, these developments look to develop a common verifiable cognizance that supports their story of a brought together and uncommon country.

The flood of nationalistic opinions has suggestions for global relations, as countries explore an inexorably mind boggling international scene. Patriot pioneers might take on emphatic international strategies, focusing on the apparent interests of their country over cooperative global endeavors. Strategy can turn out to be more conditional, with an emphasis on two-sided arrangements that focus on prompt public increases. The ascent of patriot feelings challenges the customary standards of global collaboration and discretion, presenting a component of flightiness and a potential shift away from multilateralism.

While the flood of nationalistic opinions is frequently connected with right-inclining political developments, it isn't bound to a particular philosophical range. Components of patriotism can be tracked down across the political range, adjusting to various settings and answering differed concerns.

Now and again, left-inclining patriot developments might zero in on monetary equity, social fairness, and hostile to globalization, featuring the different manners by which patriot feelings can show.

The flood of nationalistic opinions isn't uniform across all countries, and its effect differs in view of authentic, social, and political settings. In certain locales, patriot developments have acquired huge political impact, molding strategy choices and public talk. In others, the flood of nationalistic opinions might be more quelled, with countries underscoring the significance of worldwide coordinated effort and collaboration.

The peculiarity of the flood of nationalistic opinions likewise brings up basic issues about the harmony between public pride and comprehensive administration. While a solid feeling of public character can cultivate solidarity and metro pride, an exclusionary type of patriotism that minimizes specific gatherings can prompt disruptiveness and social pressure. Countries are entrusted with exploring this sensitive equilibrium, encouraging a feeling of having a place without surrendering to exclusionary rehearses that sabotage social union.

2.2 Changes in Immigration Policies

Changes in migration strategies have arisen as an unmistakable and dynamic part of the developing worldwide scene, reflecting moving political, monetary, and social elements. Countries all over the planet are rethinking their ways to deal with migration, wrestling with the intricacies of segment shifts, monetary necessities, and advancing thoughts of public character. The progressions in movement strategies unfurl against a setting of uplifted discussions, polarization, and the crossing point of helpful worries with public interests.

Monetary contemplations assume a urgent part in forming changes in migration strategies. Numerous countries perceive the job of migrants in adding to financial development, advancement, and work market elements. As worldwide economies go through changes, nations are changing their movement strategies to draw in gifted laborers, business visionaries, and abilities that line up with their financial requirements. The accentuation on abilities and commitments to the work market turns into a critical model in migration strategy changes.

Alternately, monetary difficulties and worries about work relocation can set off more prohibitive migration measures. During times of monetary slumps or high joblessness, a few countries might fix movement strategies to address homegrown worries. The discernment that outsiders might vie for occupations and strain social administrations can prompt the execution of stricter passage prerequisites and impediments on the quantity of workers conceded.

Changes in migration arrangements are additionally affected by moving segment designs. Maturing populaces in a few created countries provoke an interest for more youthful specialists to help benefits frameworks and support financial efficiency. Accordingly, migration approaches might be adjusted to draw in more youthful transients who can add to the labor force and reduce segment lopsided characteristics. On the other hand, worries about segment shifts and social personality can fuel prohibitive migration measures, especially in countries where nerves about osmosis or social protection are articulated.

Security contemplations, especially in the outcome of worldwide occasions, for example, fear monger assaults, have fundamentally affected changes in migration arrangements. Countries might carry out stricter reviewing methodology, improved record verifications, and expanded line safety efforts to relieve apparent security gambles related with movement. The conflation of migration with public safety has prompted the prioritization of line control and the improvement of strategies pointed toward forestalling potential security dangers.

Compassionate contemplations likewise shape changes in movement strategies, especially in light of worldwide emergencies like contentions, abuse, and catastrophic events. Countries frequently change their arrangements to oblige exiles and shelter searchers, perceiving the ethical basic to give security and backing to those escaping desperate conditions. Nonetheless, changes in popular assessment and political environments can impact the eagerness of countries to broaden compassionate guide through their migration approaches, prompting varieties in reactions to evacuee emergencies.

The political scene assumes a critical part in molding changes in movement strategies. The ascent of egalitarian developments and patriot feelings in different regions of the planet has provoked a reexamination of movement structures. Egalitarian pioneers might advocate for more prohibitive movement measures, outlining migration as a danger to public personality, culture, or financial prosperity. The politicization of migration issues can bring about the execution of approaches that line up with egalitarian accounts, affecting the encounters of migrants and molding public insights.

The idea of boundary control and the administration of movement streams are focal subjects in changes to migration arrangements. Countries might take on strategies pointed toward bracing lines, executing stricter visa prerequisites, and upgrading requirement components to control the section and home of outsiders. The attention on line control reflects worries about sway, security, and the craving to deal with the segment creation of the populace.

Global joint efforts and arrangements likewise impact changes in movement approaches. Respective and multilateral arrangements, like territorial monetary organizations, can work with the development of individuals across borders.

Alternately, international pressures and stressed global relations might lead countries to reevaluate their responsibilities to such arrangements, bringing about approach moves that influence the portability of people and the acknowledgment of unfamiliar qualifications.

The combination of innovation into movement strategies is a prominent contemporary turn of events. Progressed biometric frameworks, information examination, and man-made reasoning are progressively utilized to smooth out movement processes, upgrade safety efforts, and oversee relocation streams. While mechanical headways offer effectiveness and exactness, they additionally raise worries about protection, information security, and the potential for biased works on, provoking continuous discussions about the moral ramifications of innovation in migration approaches.

The Coronavirus pandemic has acquainted phenomenal difficulties and intricacies with migration approaches. General wellbeing concerns have prompted the execution of movement limitations, line terminations, and quarantine measures to control the spread of the infection. The pandemic has highlighted the interconnectedness of worldwide wellbeing and relocation, provoking countries to reevaluate their availability to answer wellbeing crises and the effect of portability on general wellbeing.

Social and social elements add to changes in movement strategies, reflecting developing mentalities toward variety, consideration, and multiculturalism. Cultural discussions about social personality, osmosis, and the combination of workers shape strategy choices. The acknowledgment of variety as a strength and a resource might prompt strategies that focus on inclusivity and social pluralism, while worries about friendly union and the conservation of public character might provoke arrangements that underline osmosis and social arrangement.

Changes in migration arrangements likewise influence the encounters of undocumented workers. Stricter requirement measures, expanded line security, and an emphasis on removal can prompt increased weaknesses for undocumented people. Alternately, strategy changes that give pathways to lawful status, regularization, or reprieve can essentially affect the existences of undocumented outsiders, impacting their admittance to privileges, potential open doors, and social coordination.

The talk on changes in migration approaches is intrinsically attached to moral contemplations and common freedoms. The treatment of travelers, exiles, and shelter searchers brings up issues about the honest convictions of countries, the adherence to global philanthropic standards, and the moral ramifications of approaches that might bring about the underestimation or abuse of weak populaces. Banters about the moral components of migration strategies highlight the requirement for a harmony between public interests and a pledge to common freedoms.

2.3 Impact on Global Diplomacy

The developing scene of worldwide strategy is going through significant changes, impacted by a huge number of elements that reach from international movements and mechanical progressions to the elements of worldwide emergencies. This intricate exchange of powers is reshaping the manner in which countries draw in with one another, modifying customary strategic standards, and presenting new difficulties and amazing open doors. As we dive into the effect on worldwide strategy, it becomes evident that the conventional standards are giving way to a more interconnected and dynamic conciliatory climate.

One of the critical drivers of progress in worldwide tact is the moving international scene. Conventional power elements are being tested as arising economies champion themselves on the worldwide stage, and laid out powers wrestle with changing ranges of prominence. The ascent of provincial powers, like China and India, has prompted a multipolar world where conciliatory commitment are portrayed by a more extensive cluster of entertainers with different interests and points of view. This requires a re-calibration of political systems to oblige a more intricate and decentralized worldwide power structure.

Innovative headways significantly affect worldwide discretion, presenting the two difficulties and open doors. The advanced age has changed the manner in which countries convey, direct tact, and draw in with their residents and the global local area. Virtual entertainment stages, for example, have become amazing assets for public discretion, empowering pioneers to discuss straightforwardly with worldwide crowds and shape public discernments. In any case, the speed and spread of data in the advanced period additionally present difficulties, with deception and digital dangers becoming critical contemplations in conciliatory relations.

Worldwide emergencies, for example, the Coronavirus pandemic, environmental change, and monetary vulnerabilities, have become characterizing highlights of the contemporary political scene. These emergencies rise above public lines, requiring cooperative and composed discretionary endeavors. The reaction to the pandemic, for instance, featured the significance of global collaboration in regions like general wellbeing, antibody dispersion, and financial recuperation. Tact is progressively called upon to address shared difficulties that require aggregate arrangements, building up the interconnectedness of the worldwide local area.

The ascent of non-state entertainers and transnational issues has added a layer of intricacy to worldwide strategy. Non-administrative associations (NGOs), worldwide partnerships, and global associations assume persuasive parts in molding conciliatory plans. Issues, for example, basic freedoms, environmental change, and worldwide wellbeing require conciliatory commitment that goes past customary state-to-state associations. Negotiators should explore a scene where numerous partners add to dynamic cycles, impacting worldwide standards and strategies.

Financial contemplations have become indispensable to discretionary procedures, as countries perceive the interconnectedness of their monetary prosperity with worldwide business sectors. Economic alliance, venture organizations, and monetary unions are pivotal parts of present day discretion. The monetary aspect impacts strategic choices, exchanges, and partnerships, as countries look to defend their financial advantages and explore the intricacies of a globalized commercial center.

The job of strategy in addressing security challenges has developed because of new and arising dangers. Conventional security concerns, like military contentions and regional questions, continue, yet modern dangers, including digital fighting, illegal intimidation, and unbalanced fighting, have acquired conspicuousness. Strategy is progressively entrusted with finding political answers for these complicated security challenges, underlining struggle anticipation, de-acceleration, and global participation in tending to shared security concerns.

Delicate power, social discretion, and public tact have become fundamental apparatuses in molding worldwide discernments and affecting global relations. Countries perceive the significance of extending a positive picture to improve their impact and fabricate worldwide unions. Social trades, instructive organizations, and individuals to-individuals discretion add to cultivating common comprehension and building spans between countries. The capacity to use delicate power really has turned into a basic part of strategic impact in the contemporary world.

Environment strategy has arisen as a point of convergence in worldwide discretionary endeavors, mirroring the critical need to address environmental change and natural supportability. Peaceful accords, like the Paris Understanding, highlight the cooperative idea of environment strategy. Countries take part in conciliatory exchanges to set discharge decrease targets, advance clean energy drives, and address the effects of environmental change. Environment tact mirrors the acknowledgment that natural difficulties require facilitated worldwide activity and discretionary endeavors to get responsibilities from countries around the world.

The Assembled Countries (UN) and other worldwide foundations keep on assuming a focal part in worldwide strategy, filling in as discussions for discretionary discourse, compromise, and collaboration. The adequacy of these organizations, notwithstanding, is dependent upon the eagerness of part states to take part in political cycles and comply with global standards. The difficulties looked by the UN, including international contentions and inquiries of institutional change, feature the advancing idea of multilateral tact.

Patriotism and egalitarian developments have brought new elements into worldwide tact, testing the standards of global collaboration and multilateralism. Pioneers who embrace patriot plans might focus on one-sided approaches, stating public interests over cooperative endeavors. Egalitarian developments can impact general assessment and shape discretionary needs, adding to a more conditional and nationalistic way to deal with worldwide relations.

Worldwide political endeavors have likewise been influenced by a resurgence of incredible power rivalry. Strains between significant powers, like the US, China, and Russia, have molded strategic elements and added to a more serious and self-assured international climate. The essential contest stretches out past conventional conciliatory channels, incorporating financial, innovative, and military aspects, and requires skilled political systems to oversee and relieve possible contentions.

The idea of computerized tact has acquired noticeable quality, mirroring the incorporation of innovation into conciliatory practices. Online entertainment stages, computerized specialized devices, and information investigation have become basic to conciliatory effort, data spread, and public commitment. Advanced discretion permits countries to discuss straightforwardly with worldwide crowds, shape stories, and answer developing occasions progressively. Be that as it may, it additionally acquaints difficulties related with network safety, disinformation, and the moral utilization of innovation in conciliatory endeavors.

Discretion in the 21st century requires versatility, development, and an acknowledgment of the interconnected idea of worldwide difficulties. The effect on worldwide discretion is portrayed by a takeoff from conventional standards, the coordination of innovation into political practices, and a shift towards additional cooperative and comprehensive methodologies. As countries explore the intricacies of the contemporary conciliatory scene, the capacity to offset public interests with worldwide obligations, influence delicate power really, and participate in political endeavors that address shared difficulties will be significant for encouraging global collaboration and keeping up with steadiness in an undeniably related world.

Chapter 3

The Rise of Technological Governance

The ascent of mechanical administration denotes an extraordinary change in the manner social orders are made due, choices are made, and strategies are carried out. As we explore the intricacies of the 21st 100 years, mechanical headways have become essential to administration structures, offering phenomenal instruments for proficiency, availability, and information driven navigation. This shift, notwithstanding, brings up significant issues about the harmony between mechanical development and popularity based values, the moral ramifications of innovative administration, and the potential for new types of force and control.

One of the characterizing elements of mechanical administration is the usage of trend setting innovations to smooth out managerial cycles, upgrade public administrations, and further develop generally administration effectiveness.

Legislatures all over the planet are progressively utilizing computerized reasoning (artificial intelligence), information investigation, and computerization to streamline works like public assistance conveyance, policing, administrative cycles. This innovative mix intends to upgrade the responsiveness of government establishments, diminish administrative obstacles, and give residents more consistent and customized administrations.

Information driven administration is a focal part of innovative administration, depending on tremendous measures of data gathered from different sources to illuminate strategy choices. The utilization of large information and examination permits state run administrations to distinguish patterns, evaluate public requirements, and allot assets all the more really. From metropolitan intending to medical services the board, information driven administration vows to improve dynamic cycles, advance asset allotment, and address cultural difficulties with more prominent accuracy.

Shrewd urban communities address an unmistakable sign of innovative administration, where interconnected frameworks and Web of Things (IoT) gadgets are utilized to screen and oversee metropolitan foundation. From traffic the executives and energy utilization to garbage removal, these shrewd frameworks mean to make more reasonable, proficient, and bearable metropolitan conditions. In any case, the organization of such advances likewise raises worries about security, observation, and the potential for abuse of gathered information.

Innovative administration stretches out past the domain of managerial proficiency and metropolitan wanting to envelop political independent direction. E-administration stages, internet casting a ballot frameworks, and computerized resident commitment drives are turning out to be more common, promising to improve majority rule cycles and increment urban investment. These innovations can possibly make administration more open, straightforward, and comprehensive, permitting residents to draw in with the political cycle from the solace of their homes.

The ascent of innovative administration is firmly entwined with the more extensive digitization of economies. Web based business, advanced finance, and online assistance stages are reshaping the monetary scene, provoking states to adjust administrative structures to these developing real factors. The coordination of blockchain innovation, for example, is modifying conventional ways to deal with monetary exchanges, store network the board, and record-keeping. States are confronted with the assignment of exploring these innovative disturbances while guaranteeing the soundness and security of their economies.

In the midst of the commitments of productivity and advancement, mechanical administration likewise presents critical difficulties and moral contemplations. One key concern is the potential for the advanced gap to fuel existing social imbalances.

As states put resources into cutting edge innovations, there is a gamble that specific sections of the populace might be abandoned because of restricted admittance to computerized foundation, computerized education, or financial variations. Guaranteeing that the advantages of innovative administration are fairly circulated turns into an essential part of capable execution.

The assortment and usage of huge measures of individual information for administration purposes bring up basic issues about security and individual privileges. The extensive reach of reconnaissance innovations, facial acknowledgment frameworks, and information examination capacities can encroach upon residents' protection in the event that not joined by hearty lawful structures and defends. Adjusting the requirement for information driven decision-production with the security of individual privileges turns into a sensitive errand for legislatures embracing innovative administration.

The ascent of mechanical administration likewise presents worries about algorithmic predisposition and dynamic straightforwardness. As computer based intelligence frameworks assume an undeniably unmistakable part in administration processes, there is a gamble that these calculations might sustain or try and worsen existing predispositions in regions like law enforcement, work, and social administrations. Guaranteeing reasonableness, responsibility, and straightforwardness in algorithmic navigation becomes fundamental to forestall unseen side-effects and alleviate the potential for separation.

The convergence of mechanical power in the possession of a couple of enterprises brings up issues about the impact of private elements in forming administration structures. Tech monsters with admittance to tremendous measures of client information and cutting edge innovations can use critical impact over political, financial, and social cycles. State run administrations should wrestle with the need to direct these elements to forestall maltreatments of force while cultivating a climate that empowers advancement and financial development.

Network safety turns into a vital worry in the time of mechanical administration. As legislatures progressively depend on computerized frameworks to oversee basic foundation and delicate data, the weakness to digital dangers heightens. Guaranteeing the versatility of computerized framework, shielding against cyberattacks, and creating successful reaction instruments become basic to keep up with the honesty and security of innovative administration.

Worldwide joint effort and the advancement of worldwide administration structures are fundamental parts of tending to the difficulties presented by innovative administration. As innovations rise above public lines, there is a requirement for shared standards, principles, and arrangements to direct the mindful utilization of trend setting innovations. Cooperative endeavors can assist with forestalling a divided and disconnected way to deal with innovative administration, cultivating a more durable and internationally adjusted system.

The ascent of mechanical administration meets with more extensive discussions about the idea of a majority rule government and the job of residents in dynamic cycles. While innovative progressions offer the possibility to upgrade vote based rehearses through expanded investment and straightforwardness, there is likewise a gamble of technocracy — an administration model where choices are driven by specialized specialists as opposed to chose delegates. Finding some kind of harmony between innovative productivity and majority rule values turns into a focal test for legislatures embracing mechanical administration.

Moral contemplations in mechanical administration reach out past issues of security and algorithmic predisposition. The capable turn of events and sending of arising advancements, like biotechnology, computerized reasoning, and independent frameworks, require moral structures that address possible dangers and guarantee that these innovations line up with cultural qualities. Laying out moral rules becomes fundamental to forestall potentially negative results and guarantee that innovative progressions contribute emphatically to human prosperity.

The ascent of mechanical administration prompts a reconsideration of conventional administration models and the job of residents in forming the fate of their social orders. As legislatures embrace cutting edge innovations to upgrade proficiency and dynamic cycles, there is a requirement for proactive public talk, commitment, and instruction. Guaranteeing that residents are educated, involved, and have a voice in the reception of mechanical administration measures becomes pivotal to keeping up with the popularity based rules that support present day cultures.

3.1 Accelerated Technological Integration

The peculiarity of sped up innovative mix is reshaping the texture of social orders, economies, and the worldwide scene at an exceptional speed. As we explore the intricacies of the 21st hundred years, the union of arising advancements is catalyzing extraordinary changes across different areas. From man-made brainpower (simulated intelligence) and the Web of Things (IoT) to biotechnology and quantum registering, the collaboration of these innovations is making a dynamic and interconnected biological system that has expansive ramifications for people, organizations, and countries.

One of the characterizing parts of sped up mechanical reconciliation is the unavoidable impact of man-made reasoning. Artificial intelligence, incorporating AI, normal language handling, and PC vision, is driving headways across different areas. From independent vehicles and prescient examination to customized medical care and remote helpers, man-made intelligence is at the bleeding edge of advancement. The capacity of computer based intelligence frameworks to break down huge datasets, perceive examples, and go with complex choices is reforming ventures, changing how assignments are performed, and enlarging human abilities.

The Web of Things (IoT) is one more basic part of sped up innovative coordination. The interconnection of gadgets, sensors, and regular items through the web is making an organized environment that empowers consistent correspondence and information trade. Savvy homes, modern mechanization, and associated urban communities are unmistakable indications of IoT applications. The reconciliation of IoT improves productivity and comfort as well as brings up issues about information security, protection, and the moral ramifications of unavoidable network.

Biotechnology is encountering exceptional development and combination into different areas, going from medical care and horticulture to energy and ecological preservation. Propels in genomics, quality altering, and engineered science are opening additional opportunities for customized medication, accuracy farming, and the improvement of supportable biofuels. The combination of biotechnology with other arising innovations enhances its effect, making collaborations that hold the possibility to address complex difficulties, for example, environmental change and medical services differences.

Quantum processing, albeit still in the beginning phases of improvement, addresses a change in outlook in computational capacities. The standards of quantum mechanics, bridled for the purpose of figuring, empower the handling of huge measures of information at speeds unreachable by old style PCs. As quantum figuring develops, it can possibly change fields like cryptography, enhancement, and complex recreations. The coordination of quantum processing into existing innovative foundations could reclassify the restrictions of computational power and critical thinking.

The sped up mix of innovation is driving huge changes in the labor force and work scene. Mechanization, powered by headways in mechanical technology and artificial intelligence, is changing ventures, computerizing routine undertakings, and enlarging human work. The approach of Industry 4.0, portrayed by savvy assembling and digitalization, is reshaping creation cycles and supply chains. While these innovative headways improve effectiveness and efficiency, they likewise raise worries about work removal, the requirement for reskilling, and the expected cultural effects of a quickly developing work market.

The change of medical care through mechanical joining is clear in the improvement of accuracy medication, telehealth, and wearable wellbeing gadgets. The union of simulated intelligence, genomics, and large information investigation empowers customized treatment plans, early illness location, and more proficient medical services conveyance. Telehealth stages, worked with by network and computerized specialized apparatuses, offer distant clinical counsels and observing, growing admittance to medical care administrations. Wearable gadgets, outfitted with sensors and man-made intelligence calculations, enable people to follow their wellbeing measurements, cultivating a shift towards proactive and customized health.

In the domain of money, fintech advancements driven by mechanical mix are reshaping customary banking and monetary administrations. Blockchain innovation, known for its decentralized and secure nature, supports digital currencies and can possibly reform monetary exchanges, decreasing the dependence on middle people. Versatile banking applications, computerized wallets, and contactless installment frameworks epitomize the shift towards a more digitized and open monetary biological system. The joining of fintech improves accommodation as well as acquaints new difficulties related with network safety, administrative structures, and the potential for monetary avoidance.

The instructive scene is encountering a change in perspective with the coordination of innovation. Web based learning stages, virtual homerooms, and instructive applications influence availability to give open and customized opportunities for growth. The gamification of training, expanded reality (AR), and augmented reality (VR) advancements upgrade commitment and make learning more intuitive. In any case, the computerized partition stays a test, as differences in admittance to innovation and the web can worsen instructive disparities.

The interconnected idea of innovation is encouraging an information driven economy where data is a significant item. Huge information examination, filled by the wealth of computerized data, empowers associations to infer experiences, go with informed choices, and gain an upper hand. Information driven plans of action, customized promoting techniques, and designated publicizing epitomize the extraordinary effect of information investigation on businesses. In any case, the moral ramifications of information assortment, security concerns, and the mindful utilization of individual data are basic contemplations in the period of sped up mechanical reconciliation.

The extraordinary force of innovation stretches out past individual areas to impact the structure holding the system together and administration structures. States are utilizing innovation for e-administration drives, computerized resident commitment, and information driven approach choices. Savvy urban areas, outfitted with associated framework and IoT gadgets, expect to upgrade metropolitan living, further develop asset effectiveness, and address supportability challenges. Notwithstanding, the reconciliation of innovation into administration additionally brings up issues about information protection, observation, and the potential for innovation driven dictatorship.

Online protection turns into a central worry in the time of sped up mechanical joining. The rising interconnectivity of gadgets, frameworks, and basic foundation hoists the gamble of digital dangers and assaults. Getting networks, shielding delicate data, and creating vigorous network safety measures are basic to alleviate the expected outcomes of digital dangers on people, organizations, and countries.

The moral components of sped up mechanical combination are basic to forming dependable development. Issues like algorithmic predisposition, the moral utilization of simulated intelligence, and the possible cultural effects of innovative headways require cautious thought. Creating moral structures, cultivating straightforwardness, and participating openly talk are fundamental parts of guaranteeing that mechanical combination lines up with human qualities, regards individual freedoms, and contributes emphatically to cultural prosperity.

The worldwide scene of international relations is additionally impacted by innovative coordination. Mechanical ability has turned into a vital determinant of international impact, with countries competing for initiative in regions, for example, computer based intelligence, quantum figuring, and network protection. The race for mechanical matchless quality brings up issues about global coordinated effort, principles, and the potential for international pressures in the domain of arising advancements.

Ecological maintainability is a basic thought in the time of sped up mechanical reconciliation. While innovation can possibly address ecological difficulties through developments, for example, clean energy advances and supportable farming practices, it likewise adds to issues like electronic waste and energy utilization. Finding some kind of harmony between innovative advancement and natural stewardship becomes basic to guarantee a supportable and strong future.

3.2 Surveillance State and Privacy Concerns

The development of the observation state, described by broad checking, information assortment, and reconnaissance advancements, has raised significant security concerns, reshaping the elements between people, legislatures, and innovation. In the 21st hundred years, progressions in reconnaissance capacities, filled by computerized advances, have changed the scene of protection, prompting a fragile harmony between security goals and individual opportunities.

One of the critical drivers behind the reconnaissance state is the multiplication of observation innovations, going from omnipresent CCTV cameras to modern facial acknowledgment frameworks. Legislatures, policing, and confidential elements progressively send these advancements to screen public spaces, track people, and investigate standards of conduct. While the expected objectives frequently incorporate improving public security, forestalling wrongdoing, and countering illegal intimidation, the unavoidable idea of reconnaissance brings up issues about the limits of protection and the potential for inappropriate interruptions into people's lives.

The appearance of advanced correspondence innovations has additionally intensified the extent of reconnaissance. State run administrations and knowledge offices participate in mass observation programs, checking electronic correspondences, web exercises, and virtual entertainment cooperations. The support frequently rotates around public safety worries, determined to recognize and forestalling expected dangers. Nonetheless, the sweeping reach of these reconnaissance drives raises worries about the disintegration of security, the chilling impact on free articulation, and the potential for maltreatment of force.

The reconciliation of observation advances into day to day existence stretches out past the actual domain to the computerized circle. Advancements like facial acknowledgment, biometric information assortment, and geolocation following empower the consistent checking of people. While these advancements offer comfort and proficiency in different applications, from opening cell phones to air terminal security, they likewise present critical dangers to protection. Facial acknowledgment, specifically, has started banters about its precision, potential for abuse, and the requirement for administrative structures to oversee its arrangement.

The adaptation of individual information by tech organizations has additionally filled worries about protection in the computerized age. The broad information assortment practices of online stages, virtual entertainment organizations, and advanced specialist co-ops make itemized profiles of people's inclinations, ways of behaving, and associations. This information is frequently utilized for designated promoting, algorithmic navigation, and impacting client conduct. The commodification of individual data brings up moral issues about informed assent, client independence, and the requirement for vigorous information assurance guidelines.

Security concerns are not restricted to cooperations with innovation stages however reach out to government observation programs and the disintegration of legitimate insurances. Mass reconnaissance drives, frequently led assuming some pretense of counterterrorism endeavors, have provoked banters about the compromise among security and common freedoms. The disclosures of mass reconnaissance programs by government organizations, as exemplified by Edward Snowden's exposures, lighted worldwide conversations about the harmony between public safety objectives and the right to security.

The reconnaissance state's effect on protection isn't uniform across purviews, prompting different methodologies and lawful structures. A few nations have executed severe information security regulations, like the Overall Information Assurance Guideline (GDPR) in the European Association, to protect people's protection privileges. Others might have more lenient systems, considering broad reconnaissance with less balanced governance. This variety in approaches highlights the worldwide idea of protection concerns and the requirement for global collaboration to address the difficulties presented by the observation state.

Notwithstanding state-supported reconnaissance, the ascent of private observation additionally adds to the disintegration of security. Organizations and associations convey reconnaissance advances in the working environment, public spaces, and, surprisingly, local locations. The utilization of reconnaissance cameras, worker checking programming, and information examination in business settings raises worries about the meddlesome idea of observation past the public area. Adjusting the real interests of organizations with the privileges of people to protection turns into an essential thought in exploring this perplexing landscape.

The disintegration of security in the reconnaissance state has suggestions for popularity based social orders and individual opportunities. A key concern is the potential for a chilling impact on free discourse and political contradiction. The consciousness of being under consistent reconnaissance might dissuade people from offering contradicting viewpoints, participating in activism, or addressing authority. This self-control has repercussions for the liveliness of vote based talk and the capacity of residents to consider legislatures responsible.

The potential for maltreatment of observation abilities by specialists represents a huge danger to common freedoms. History has shown examples where reconnaissance apparatuses planned for authentic purposes have been abused for political constraint, social control, or separation. The absence of powerful oversight, straightforwardness, and responsibility instruments worsens the gamble of misuses, prompting what is going on where people might be designated in view of their convictions, affiliations, or qualities.

Protection concerns cross with more extensive discussions about the morals of computerized reasoning and mechanized independent direction. The utilization of calculations in observation, prescient policing, and risk appraisal presents predispositions and supports existing disparities. Calculations may unintentionally propagate oppression certain segment gatherings, enhancing social predispositions present in preparing information. The absence of straightforwardness in algorithmic dynamic cycles brings difficulties up in considering frameworks responsible for likely unfair results.

Because of the developing worries about protection in the reconnaissance state, there is a call for vigorous legitimate structures, moral rules, and worldwide participation. Protection regulations need to advance to address the difficulties presented by new innovations and guarantee that people have command over their own information. Endeavors to lay out clear standards for the sending of observation innovations, control information assortment rehearses, and maintain straightforwardness can assist with finding some kind of harmony between security necessities and individual protection freedoms.

Straightforwardness and responsibility are fundamental parts in alleviating the dangers related with observation. Legislatures and confidential substances sending reconnaissance advances ought to be straightforward about their capacities, targets, and the extent of information assortment. Powerful oversight systems, free administrative bodies, and legal survey assume a urgent part in guaranteeing that reconnaissance exercises stick to lawful guidelines and regard security privileges.

Mechanical arrangements that focus on security by plan and consolidate encryption, anonymization, and client assent instruments can add to shielding people's protection. Security upgrading advancements offer inventive ways to deal with safeguard delicate data while taking into consideration authentic purposes of information. Empowering the turn of events and reception of such advancements becomes basic in the mission to moderate security worries in the reconnaissance state.

Public mindfulness and schooling about security freedoms and the ramifications of observation are critical in enabling people to settle on informed decisions. Protection education programs, backing endeavors, and local area commitment drives can encourage a superior comprehension of the dangers and compromises related with observation innovations. Informed residents are better situated to request responsibility, advocate for security insurances, and add to molding dependable approaches.

Worldwide collaboration is essential in tending to the worldwide idea of security worries in the reconnaissance state. Cooperative endeavors to lay out normal guidelines, share best practices, and direction reactions to transnational reconnaissance dangers can add to a more complete and powerful methodology. Strategic drives, multilateral arrangements, and discussions for discourse can work with a mutual perspective of the difficulties presented by the reconnaissance state and the requirement for aggregate activity.

3.3 Technological Diplomacy

Mechanical strategy, a quickly developing feature of worldwide relations, highlights the convergence of innovation and tact in forming worldwide elements. In the 21st hundred years, headways in innovation have become vital to conciliatory systems, affecting the manner in which countries draw in with one another, address worldwide difficulties, and try to propel their inclinations on the world stage. Mechanical strategy includes an expansive range of exercises, going from cooperative exploration drives to network safety arrangements, mirroring the complex effect of innovation on the conciliatory scene.

One of the essential components of innovative strategy is the quest for mechanical participation and coordinated effort between countries. Perceiving the extraordinary force of innovation, nations take part in joint innovative work drives, scholarly trades, and innovation move arrangements to outfit aggregate ability. Cooperative ventures in regions like space investigation, environmentally friendly power, and man-made consciousness represent the potential for mechanical strategy to encourage advancement, address shared difficulties, and reinforce conciliatory ties.

The computerized age has changed the idea of correspondence in strategy, with innovation filling in as an impetus for improved network and data trade. Computerized strategy, frequently alluded to as e-discretion, use advanced specialized instruments, web-based entertainment stages, and online stages to work with conciliatory commitment. Pioneers and representatives utilize online entertainment channels to discuss straightforwardly with worldwide crowds, shape public stories, and take part progressively discretion. Computerized tact empowers a more straightforward and quick type of correspondence, rising above conventional political channels and contacting a different and worldwide crowd.

Mechanical strategy assumes a pivotal part in tending to worldwide difficulties that rise above public boundaries. Issues, for example, environmental change, general well-being emergencies, and online protection dangers require cooperative and facilitated discretionary endeavors. Peaceful accords and associations, for example, the Paris Settlement on environmental change or cooperative reactions to worldwide pandemics, epitomize how countries meet up to use innovation in tending to shared difficulties. Innovative arrangements, information sharing instruments, and joint examination drives become fundamental parts of discretionary procedures pointed toward handling complex worldwide issues.

Online protection has arisen as a conspicuous and squeezing part of innovative strategy. As social orders become more interconnected and dependent on computerized foundation, the dangers of digital dangers, assaults, and reconnaissance raise. Strategy assumes a basic part in laying out standards, rules, and arrangements that oversee dependable conduct in the internet. Network safety exchanges, respective arrangements, and global drives look to address the difficulties presented by malevolent digital exercises, safeguard basic framework, and cultivate participation in upgrading online protection abilities.

The job of innovation in monetary strategy is central, with countries perceiving the vital association between financial interests and mechanical headways. Economic alliance, speculation associations, and innovation related joint efforts add to the monetary element of mechanical strategy. Countries look to situate themselves as pioneers in arising advancements, encouraging development, and making good circumstances for monetary development. Mechanical seriousness turns into a vital figure molding financial connections and impacting worldwide monetary elements.

The appearance of arising advancements, for example, man-made brainpower, quantum figuring, and biotechnology, acquaints new aspects with innovative strategy. Countries vie for administration in these boondocks advancements, perceiving the key and monetary benefits they present. Strategic endeavors are coordinated towards cultivating development biological systems, drawing in ability, and laying out administrative structures that offset mechanical progressions with moral contemplations. The race for mechanical incomparability impacts international elements and shapes strategic needs.

The computerized partition, the hole between the people who approach data and correspondence advances and the people who don't, is a huge thought in mechanical strategy. Crossing over the computerized partition turns into a political basic to guarantee fair admittance to the advantages of innovation, cultivate comprehensive turn of events, and lessen worldwide inconsistencies. Strategic drives might remember joint efforts for computerized foundation projects, limit building projects, and endeavors to stretch out web availability to underserved areas.

The moral elements of innovative tact come to the bleeding edge as countries explore the mindful turn of events and sending of arising advancements. Inquiries regarding information protection, algorithmic predisposition, and the cultural effects of innovation require conciliatory commitment to lay out moral rules and administrative structures. Cooperative endeavors to address moral contemplations add to building trust, alleviating gambles, and guaranteeing that innovative headways line up with shared values.

Space tact addresses an extraordinary part of mechanical discretion, with countries taking part in cooperative space investigation, satellite send-offs, and global space arrangements. The serene utilization of space, the anticipation of room trash, and the investigation of heavenly bodies include conciliatory endeavors to lay out standards and rules overseeing space exercises. The potential for mechanical headways in space investigation to help humankind all in all highlights the cooperative idea of room tact.

Innovative tact isn't restricted to connections between country states yet additionally includes commitment with non-state entertainers, including innovation organizations, research foundations, and common society associations. Public-private associations, scholastic joint efforts, and commitment with non-legislative elements add to the more extensive scene of mechanical tact. These coordinated efforts bring assorted viewpoints, skill, and assets into discretionary drives, mirroring the undeniably decentralized nature of worldwide mechanical development.

The job of global associations in mechanical tact is huge, with substances like the Assembled Countries (UN), the Worldwide Telecom Association (ITU), and the World Wellbeing Association (WHO) filling in as discussions for strategic discourse and collaboration.

Multilateral commitment on issues like web administration, worldwide wellbeing, and standard-setting for arising advancements give roads to countries to arrange their strategic endeavors and address normal difficulties.

International pressures and contest in the mechanical space add a layer of intricacy to mechanical tact. The essential significance of advancements, for example, 5G organizations and man-made consciousness, raises worries about public safety, financial intensity, and mechanical conditions. Political endeavors expect to explore these strains, encourage worldwide participation, and forestall the discontinuity of the worldwide mechanical scene.

The fate of mechanical tact will be formed by progressing advancements in arising advances, the developing idea of worldwide difficulties, and the international elements of the computerized age. As countries keep on exploring the intricacies of innovative discretion, the capacity to work out some kind of harmony between public interests, moral contemplations, and cooperative endeavors will be urgent. The discretionary scene will keep on being affected by the groundbreaking force of innovation, forming the manner in which countries communicate, collaborate, and address the difficulties and chances of the mechanical period.

Chapter 4

Economic Restructuring

Monetary rebuilding, a multi-layered course of revamping and changing the central parts of an economy, has been a common peculiarity from the beginning of time. In the contemporary setting, monetary rebuilding is in many cases driven by a conversion of variables, including mechanical progressions, globalization, segment shifts, and international elements. This complicated and dynamic interaction reshapes ventures, business designs, and the in general financial scene, introducing the two difficulties and potential open doors for countries exploring the flows of progress.

One of the essential drivers of financial rebuilding in the cutting edge time is mechanical development. The quick speed of mechanical headways, especially in regions like man-made brainpower, mechanization, and digitalization, groundbreakingly affects ventures and work markets. Mechanization, for example, smoothes out creation processes, decreases work expenses, and increments effectiveness, prompting shifts in business designs and the requirement for a gifted labor force fit for exploring the computerized scene.

The ascent of the computerized economy is a critical result of mechanical driven monetary rebuilding. Internet business, advanced stages, and online administrations have become indispensable parts of present day monetary exercises. Conventional physical retail faces difficulties as customers progressively go to web based shopping. This shift influences work in the retail area as well as requires changes in supply chains, planned operations, and the ranges of abilities requested by the advancing position market.

Globalization is another vital power driving monetary rebuilding. The interconnectedness of economies through global exchange, venture, and the progression of data has sped up the development of merchandise, administrations, and capital across borders. While globalization brings valuable open doors for market development and admittance to assets, it likewise opens economies to expanded contest, expecting them to adjust and have some expertise in regions where they can keep a similar benefit.

The rebuilding of ventures because of globalization is apparent in the peculiarity of re-appropriating and offshoring. Organizations look for cost efficiencies by re-appropriating specific capabilities to nations with lower work costs. This training influences work in the nation of origin while adding to the monetary advancement of re-appropriating objections. The worldwide development of creation and administrations reshapes the dispersion of financial exercises on a worldwide scale, impacting the fortunes of both created and emerging countries.

Segment shifts assume a pivotal part in financial rebuilding, especially as maturing populaces and changing workforce elements present difficulties to conventional monetary models. The maturing labor force in many created economies presents difficulties, for example, a contracting work pool, expanded benefits liabilities, and changing utilization designs. Monetary rebuilding methodologies should address these segment difficulties, possibly prompting creative arrangements, for example, approaches empowering labor force interest among more seasoned people and outfitting the capability of arising advancements to make up for work deficiencies.

The change from assembling driven economies to support situated economies is a sign of monetary rebuilding. High level economies witness a decrease in the general significance of customary assembling areas, joined by the extension of administration enterprises like money, innovation, medical services, and schooling. This shift mirrors a more extensive pattern toward information based economies, where scholarly capital, development, and HR become essential drivers of monetary development.

Monetary rebuilding additionally includes the variation of work markets to changing ability necessities. The interest for high-gifted laborers in innovation, finance, and other information escalated areas frequently dominates the interest for low-talented positions. This makes difficulties connected with pay imbalance, as those without the fundamental abilities might confront decreased work prospects and pay stagnation.

Tending to these differences requires proactive measures like interests in schooling, preparing projects, and arrangements advancing comprehensive monetary development.

The natural aspect is progressively turning into a basic thought in financial rebuilding. The basic to address environmental change, decrease fossil fuel byproducts, and progress to supportable practices requires a change of ventures and energy frameworks. Monetary rebuilding that focuses on natural maintainability includes the reception of clean advances, sustainable power sources, and eco-accommodating creation strategies. This progress mitigates natural dangers as well as opens new roads for advancement, work creation, and supportable financial turn of events.

The job of government strategies in directing and it is principal to shape financial rebuilding. States assume a urgent part in establishing an empowering climate for organizations, cultivating development, and tending to the social effects of financial changes. Policymakers should work out some kind of harmony between advancing monetary development and it are impartially disseminated to guarantee that the advantages. Social wellbeing nets, training and retraining projects, and drives to advance business are among the approach devices utilized to explore the intricacies of monetary rebuilding.

The effect of financial rebuilding on provincial improvement is a basic thought, as it frequently prompts geographic variations regarding monetary open doors and thriving. Urbanization patterns, driven by the centralization of businesses and administrations in metropolitan habitats, can bring about provincial decay and lopsided turn of events. Tending to provincial variations requires designated strategies that advance comprehensive development, framework improvement, and the production of financial open doors in underserved regions.

The monetary area goes through huge changes during the time spent financial rebuilding. Developments in monetary innovation (fintech) and changes in shopper conduct, for example, the rising inclination for computerized installments, challenge conventional financial models. The ascent of digital currencies and blockchain innovation presents additional opportunities for monetary exchanges and brings up issues about the fate of customary banking and administrative systems.

The Coronavirus pandemic has added a layer of intricacy to the scene of financial rebuilding. The disturbances brought about by the pandemic sped up specific patterns, like remote work, web based business reception, and digitalization. All the while, areas like travel, accommodation, and conventional retail confronted phenomenal difficulties. State run administrations answered with monetary improvement measures, featuring the requirement for readiness and flexibility in policymaking during seasons of emergency.

Monetary rebuilding meets with social contemplations, impacting pay dissemination, social versatility, and by and large cultural prosperity. The potential for work dislodging because of robotization, for instance, raises worries about pay imbalance and the requirement for reskilling and upskilling projects to prepare laborers for advancing position markets. Social incorporation turns into a critical part of monetary rebuilding, underscoring the significance of guaranteeing that the advantages of financial development are shared extensively across society.

The moral components of financial rebuilding are essential to molding strategies and practices that focus on cultural prosperity. Inquiries concerning corporate obligation, fair work rehearses, and the effect of financial exercises on weak populaces highlight the requirement for a moral system to direct rebuilding endeavors. Offsetting monetary targets with moral contemplations becomes fundamental in encouraging a supportable and impartial financial future.

4.1 Shifts in Global Supply Chains

Worldwide stockpile chains, many-sided organizations of creation and dispersion that range across nations and landmasses, have been going through critical changes lately. The elements of worldwide stock chains are formed by a large number of variables, including international contemplations, mechanical headways, financial patterns, and unexpected interruptions like the Coronavirus pandemic. Understanding these movements is critical as they influence businesses, exchange connections, and the general interconnectedness of the worldwide economy.

One of the noticeable drivers of movements in worldwide stockpile chains is the developing international scene. Generally, numerous organizations laid out supply chains in view of cost contemplations, trying to exploit lower creation costs in specific districts. In any case, international pressures and exchange debates have provoked a re-examination of this methodology. The exchange struggle between the US and China, for example, prompted expanded taxes and vulnerabilities, provoking organizations to enhance their stockpile chains to moderate dangers related with international interruptions.

The Coronavirus pandemic revealed the weaknesses of worldwide inventory chains. The far and wide disturbances brought about by lockdowns, travel limitations, and disturbances to creation featured the dangers of overreliance on single-source providers and the delicacy of in the nick of time stock models. Thus, there has been a developing accentuation on building stronger stockpile chains that can endure shocks and interruptions. This strength incorporates differentiating providers, reexamining stock administration procedures, and consolidating computerized advances for upgraded perceivability and dexterity.

Mechanical headways, especially in computerization and digitalization, assume an extraordinary part in reshaping worldwide stockpile chains. The ascent of Industry 4.0, described by the joining of brilliant innovations, information investigation, and the Web of Things (IoT) into assembling processes, is impacting the way in which products are delivered and conveyed. Mechanization takes into account more effective and adaptable creation, decreasing the dependence on difficult work and adding to the decentralization of creation offices.

The digitalization of supply chains upgrades perceivability and straightforwardness, empowering continuous following of merchandise, stock administration, and request determining. Advances like blockchain give secure and straightforward discernibility across the store network, addressing concerns connected with validness, moral obtaining, and supportability. These innovative headways are working on functional proficiency as well as adding to the advancement of more maintainable and mindful production network rehearses.

Reshoring and regionalization are patterns arising in light of the previously mentioned difficulties and contemplations. Reshoring includes taking creation back to the nation of origin, while regionalization centers around laying out supply chains inside a particular geographic district. The inspirations driving these movements are complex. Organizations are looking to decrease lead times, lower transportation expenses, and improve inventory network perceivability by drawing creation nearer to end markets. Furthermore, reshoring and regionalization are driven by a craving to help nearby economies, answer changing shopper inclinations for supportability, and relieve international dangers related with worldwide stock chains.

Manageability contemplations are progressively affecting choices connected with worldwide stockpile chains. As attention to natural issues develops, organizations are feeling the squeeze to take on more reasonable and eco-accommodating practices. This incorporates diminishing carbon impressions, limiting waste, and guaranteeing dependable obtaining of materials. Manageable inventory network rehearses line up with corporate social obligation objectives as well as reverberate with buyers who focus on naturally cognizant items and organizations.

Economic deals and international partnerships likewise assume an essential part in molding the course of worldwide stock chains. The renegotiation of economic accords, like the US Mexico-Canada Understanding (USMCA) to supplant NAFTA, influences the terms of exchange among countries and impacts the setup of supply chains. International coalitions, for example, the European Association's endeavors to reinforce monetary ties inside the alliance, set out open doors for organizations to re-think and advance their inventory network techniques inside unambiguous locales.

The ascent of online business and changing shopper conduct are key variables affecting worldwide stockpile chains. The rising commonness of web based shopping has prompted a flood popular for fast and dependable conveyance administrations.

This shift has provoked organizations to reconfigure their stockpile chains to oblige direct-to-purchaser models and satisfy online business arranges effectively. Last-mile planned operations, warehousing, and conveyance networks are going through changes to live up to the assumptions of the present carefully associated and request-ing purchasers.

Common liberties and moral contemplations are turning out to be more basic to inventory network the executives. Buyers and administrative bodies are progressively investigating organizations for moral obtaining rehearses, fair work conditions, and adherence to basic liberties norms. This investigation has suggestions for worldwide stockpile chains, as organizations are constrained to guarantee that their providers maintain moral norms. This emphasis on moral obtaining isn't just determined by administrative tensions yet additionally mirrors a more extensive cultural mindfulness and interest for socially dependable strategic policies.

The job of states in impacting worldwide stock chains is critical. Exchange strate-gies, duties, and administrative structures set by states can either work with or block the smooth working of worldwide inventory chains. Motivations for homegrown creation, economic alliance, and international contemplations shape the choices of organizations as they explore the administrative scene. Government mediations, like commodity limitations or authorizations, can have flowing consequences for supply chains, provoking organizations to reevaluate their obtaining and dispersion systems.

The changes in worldwide stock chains have suggestions for work markets and busi-ness designs. The mechanization of assembling cycles might prompt work uprooting in specific businesses, while the development of web based business might set out new open doors in coordinated operations and appropriation. The interest for computer-ized abilities is expanding as innovation assumes a more noticeable part in production network the board. Versatility and persistent upskilling become fundamental for the labor force to stay cutthroat in a developing monetary scene.

The continuous changes in worldwide stockpile chains highlight the requirement for versatility and strength among organizations. Organizations that proactively embrace change, put resources into mechanical abilities, and focus on manageability and moral contemplations are better situated to explore the intricacies of the developing worldwide production network scene. Cooperation and data sharing across production network accomplices, alongside an emphasis on building vigorous and adaptable inventory network techniques, are key components of outcome in a period set apart by consistent change and disturbance. Fundamentally, worldwide stockpile chains are in a condition of change, driven by a conversion of elements that require a vital and forward-looking way to deal with production network the executives in the years to come.

4.2 Economic Nationalism and Protectionism

Financial patriotism and protectionism, when thought about periphery monetary philosophies, have encountered a resurgence lately, testing the well established pattern toward globalization and streamlined commerce. As countries wrestle with the intricacies of a quickly changing worldwide monetary scene, the reception of financial patriot and protectionist strategies mirrors a reconsideration of needs, a reaction to saw difficulties, and a longing to shield homegrown ventures. This resurgence conveys suggestions for worldwide exchange, conciliatory relations, and the general engineering of the worldwide economy.

Financial patriotism is a way of thinking that focuses on the interests of the country state regardless of anything else in monetary issues. It accentuates arrangements pointed toward safeguarding homegrown enterprises, guaranteeing the government assistance of the homegrown labor force, and accomplishing monetary independence. The resurgence of monetary patriotism is frequently determined by worries about the effects of globalization, including position uprooting, wage stagnation, and the disintegration of public financial power.

Protectionism, a subset of financial patriotism, includes the inconvenience of boundaries to exchange to safeguard homegrown enterprises from unfamiliar rivalry. These boundaries can appear as duties, portions, sponsorships, and other exchange limitations. The reasoning behind protectionist measures is to give homegrown ventures an upper hand, safeguard occupations, and forestall the outpouring of capital. While protectionism might offer momentary advantages to specific businesses, pundits contend that it can prompt shortcomings, diminished buyer decision, and reprisal from exchanging accomplices.

One of the vital drivers behind the resurgence of monetary patriotism and protectionism is the insight that globalization has not conveyed equally dispersed benefits. Pundits contend that the advantages of deregulation have lopsidedly gathered to worldwide partnerships and more affluent sections of society, while specific enterprises and laborers have borne the brunt of worldwide rivalry. This apparent disparity has energized a reaction against international alliances and incited requires a reexamination of exchange strategies to focus on the interests of homegrown laborers and enterprises.

The disintegration of assembling bases in a few created economies has been a point of convergence of financial patriotism. Countries that were once modern forces to be reckoned with have seen the offshoring of blue collar positions to nations with lower work costs. This pattern has prompted deindustrialization in certain districts, adding to joblessness, monetary disengagement, and a feeling of loss of public personality attached to assembling ability. The resurgence of monetary patriotism looks to switch this pattern by advancing strategies that empower the reshoring of assembling and the rejuvenation of homegrown ventures.

The political scene assumes a critical part in the resurgence of monetary patriotism. Egalitarian forerunners in different nations have benefited from the discontent with globalization and deregulation to propel their political plans. The guarantee to safeguard homegrown ventures, make occupations, and focus on public interests reverberates with portions of the populace that vibe abandoned by the powers of globalization. The political allure of monetary patriotism is obvious in the ascent of pioneers pushing for protectionist measures and a reassertion of public financial control.

The exchange pressures between the US and China have been a point of convergence of the discussion encompassing monetary patriotism and protectionism. The exchange debate, described by blow for blow levies and allegations of unreasonable exchange rehearses, reflects more extensive international strains and monetary contest between the two biggest economies. The U.S. government, under the Trump organization, sought after a protectionist plan, forcing duties on a scope of Chinese products to address apparent exchange irregular characteristics and safeguard American businesses. This methodology, while well known among certain fragments of the U.S. populace, set off worries about the potential for an exchange war and disturbances to worldwide stockpile chains.

Brexit, the Unified Realm's choice to leave the European Association, is one more indication of monetary patriotism. The craving for more prominent command over public strategies, including exchange and movement, persuaded the Brexit vote. As the UK looks to reclassify its financial associations with the EU and the remainder of the world, inquiries regarding protectionist measures, economic alliance, and the harmony between public independence and monetary combination come to the front.

The Coronavirus pandemic has added a layer of intricacy to the discussion on financial patriotism. The disturbances brought about by the pandemic, including store network interferences and deficiencies of basic products, provoked a few countries to reconsider their reliance on worldwide stockpile chains. The quest for independence in fundamental merchandise, like clinical supplies and drugs, turned into a need for certain nations. This shift toward financial strength and confidence converges with the standards of monetary patriotism and protectionism.

While financial patriotism and protectionism resound with specific fragments of the populace, pundits contend that these approaches convey dangers and disadvantages. Protectionist measures, like duties, can prompt exchange pressures, diminished worldwide monetary development, and greater expenses for buyers. Furthermore, retaliatory measures from exchanging accomplices can worsen monetary vulnerabilities. The accentuation on independence may likewise prompt shortcomings, as it could be more financially savvy for countries to spend significant time in specific enterprises and take part in worldwide stock chains.

The discussion on monetary patriotism and protectionism stretches out to the domain of financial discretion. The standards of deregulation and globalization have been fundamental to the post-The Second Great War worldwide monetary request. Foundations like the World Exchange Association (WTO) play had a focal impact in cultivating a standards based worldwide exchanging framework. The resurgence of monetary patriotism challenges these standards and establishments, bringing up issues about the eventual fate of global financial collaboration and the potential for a shift toward a more divided and reciprocal way to deal with exchange.

The effect of monetary patriotism and protectionism on worldwide stockpile chains is significant. The accentuation on reshoring and lessening reliance on unfamiliar providers has suggestions for the arrangement of supply chains. Organizations might reconsider their obtaining systems, expand providers, and embrace emergency courses of action to explore the vulnerabilities related with protectionist measures. The expanded spotlight on homegrown creation might prompt a reconsideration of cost designs, seriousness, and the general productivity of supply chains.

The future direction of financial patriotism and protectionism is dubious and dependent upon different variables, including political turns of events, monetary real factors, and international elements. While the resurgence of these philosophies mirrors a reexamination of needs in certain quarters, it likewise brings up issues about the drawn out maintainability of protectionist measures and their effect on worldwide monetary interconnectedness. Adjusting the interests of homegrown enterprises with the advantages of a universally coordinated economy represents a perplexing test for policymakers and pioneers exploring the complexities of financial patriotism in a quickly developing world.

4.3 New Economic Alliances and Strategies

In the contemporary scene of worldwide financial matters, the rise of new monetary partnerships and techniques mirrors a powerful change in global relations and exchange elements. Countries are progressively investigating different organizations, coordinated effort models, and vital systems to explore the difficulties and open doors introduced by a quickly influencing world. These developing monetary unions and procedures envelop a scope of drives, from local financial organizations to imaginative economic alliance, as countries try to get financial development, mechanical benefits, and international impact.

Local monetary organizations are a remarkable pattern in the development of new financial collusions. These organizations unite adjoining nations with shared financial interests to encourage provincial incorporation, exchange assistance, and cooperative turn of events.

Models incorporate the European Association (EU), the African Mainland Streamlined commerce Region (AfCFTA), and the Extensive and Moderate Understanding for Transoceanic Organization (CPTPP). These collusions intend to smooth out exchange, kill hindrances, and make a more interconnected and monetarily dynamic locale.

The European Association, a spearheading illustration of local financial mix, addresses a model where part states pool power in specific monetary issues to accomplish aggregate advantages. The EU works with the free development of merchandise, administrations, capital, and individuals, making a solitary market that improves monetary effectiveness and intensity. While not without challenges, the EU exhibits the potential for more profound monetary coordinated effort among countries with a common obligation to territorial mix.

The African Mainland Streamlined commerce Region is a milestone drive that tries to make a solitary market for labor and products across the African landmass. By advancing intra-African exchange, decreasing duties, and cultivating financial collaboration, AfCFTA means to open the monetary capability of the landmass and improve its worldwide intensity. The outcome of such territorial drives relies upon tending to foundation challenges, orchestrating guidelines, and building a structure for reasonable turn of events.

The Extensive and Moderate Understanding for Transoceanic Association, conceived out of the first Transoceanic Organization (TPP), addresses a monetary partnership among Pacific Edge countries. By bringing down exchange obstructions, blending guidelines, and advancing financial participation, CPTPP means to make a more coordinated and proficient exchanging coalition. The understanding features the responsibility of part countries to open business sectors and shared monetary objectives.

Notwithstanding provincial partnerships, nations are investigating inventive economic deals and techniques to encourage monetary development and intensity. Respective and multilateral economic alliance permit countries to alter their monetary connections in light of shared interests and needs. The Belt and Street Drive (BRI), proposed by China, embodies a far reaching system that joins framework improvement, exchange network, and financial collaboration to fortify China's binds with taking an interest nations.

The Belt and Street Drive, sent off in 2013, looks to make an organization of foundation projects interfacing Asia, Europe, and Africa. Through interests in ports, rail routes, energy projects, and computerized foundation, China means to upgrade shipping lanes, animate monetary turn of events, and grow its international impact.

The BRI addresses a worldview where financial interests interweave with vital international contemplations, encouraging network and collaboration across locales.

Vital associations between significant economies are additionally forming the worldwide financial scene. The US Mexico-Canada Understanding (USMCA), supplanting the North American International alliance (NAFTA), mirrors a restored way to deal with financial coordinated effort among North American neighbors. USMCA means to modernize exchange connections, address work and natural worries, and give a structure to commonly valuable financial ties.

Past conventional economic accords, the idea of financial partnerships is growing to remember joint efforts for arising fields like innovation, advancement, and environmental change. Innovation collusions are framing to advance innovative work, encourage development, and address normal difficulties. The European Association's Computerized Single Market drive, for example, tries to make a bound together advanced space that works with the free progression of information, encourages development, and upgrades advanced intensity.

In the domain of development and innovation, vital collusions are framing to use the qualities of different countries. Joint efforts in regions, for example, man-made consciousness, quantum registering, and sustainable power exhibit the acknowledgment that common innovative work endeavors can speed up mechanical headways and address worldwide difficulties. The foundation of worldwide exploration places, joint endeavors, and cooperative subsidizing components represents the developing idea of monetary unions in the innovation space.

Environmental change and maintainable improvement are progressively becoming central focuses for financial collusions. The Paris Understanding, embraced in 2015, addresses a worldwide obligation to address environmental change by and large. Countries meet up to set outflow decrease targets, share best practices, and prepare monetary assets to change toward a feasible and low-carbon future. The arrangement of monetary interests with natural maintainability highlights the significance of cooperative systems in tending to squeezing worldwide difficulties.

While financial partnerships and procedures offer open doors for development and coordinated effort, they are not without challenges. The international strains between significant powers, exchange questions, and different administrative systems can thwart the consistent working of financial partnerships. Arranging economic accords, particularly those that include a huge number of different economies, requires tending to changing interests, conquering protectionist feelings, and exploring complex international elements.

Moreover, the Coronavirus pandemic has uncovered weaknesses in worldwide stock chains, provoking countries to reexamine their financial conditions and versatility. The pandemic has prompted disturbances in exchange, featuring the requirement for expanded supply chains, upgraded computerized capacities, and a hearty structure for tending to worldwide wellbeing emergencies. The post-pandemic time underscores the significance of building financial collusions that consider strength, flexibility, and cooperative reactions to unanticipated difficulties.

Chapter 5

Social Movements and Activism

Social developments and activism, necessary parts of cultural advancement, play played critical parts in molding the course of history and driving extraordinary change. Pull in a craving for equity, balance, and the quest for common liberties, social developments are dynamic articulations of aggregate organization that challenge existing power structures, advocate for underestimated networks, and push for foundational changes. The historical backdrop of social developments is rich and various, including battles for social liberties, ladies' freedom, ecological equity, LGBTQ+ privileges, and various different causes. This investigation dives into the idea of social developments, their authentic setting, key drivers, challenges, and the advancing scene of contemporary activism.

Nature of Social Developments:
Social developments can be comprehensively characterized as coordinated, aggregate endeavors to achieve social, political, monetary, or social change. They emerge because of seen treacheries, disparities, or complaints inside a general public. While every social development is extraordinary, certain normal attributes characterize their temperament.

Right off the bat, social developments are regularly grassroots undertakings, frequently determined by conventional individuals who share a typical reason or concern. They prepare people who might be straightforwardly impacted by an issue or who relate to those confronting unfairness. Grassroots developments draw strength from the variety of their members and are frequently decentralized, depending on organizations of people, local gatherings, and associations.

Besides, social developments are dynamic and versatile. They develop because of evolving conditions, integrating groundbreaking thoughts, procedures, and innovations. Developments might move in center or expand their degree as they answer arising issues or gain a more profound comprehension of the intricacies encompassing their goal.

Thirdly, the idea of social developments is frequently diverse, perceiving the interconnectedness of different types of mistreatment. Developments progressively recognize the diversity of personalities, understanding that people might confront numerous types of segregation in view of variables like race, orientation, sexuality, and financial status.

Fourthly, social developments take part in a scope of strategies to accomplish their targets. These strategies might incorporate public fights, common insubordination, grassroots getting sorted out, legitimate support, media missions, and local area instruction. The viability of these methodologies relies upon the particular setting, the idea of the development, and the reactions of the establishments being tested.

Verifiable Setting of Social Developments:

Since the beginning of time, social developments play played instrumental parts in testing severe situation, pushing for privileges, and molding the direction of social orders. The social liberties development in the US during the 1950s and 1960s remains as a turning point, facing racial isolation and fundamental prejudice. Driven by figures like Martin Luther Lord Jr. what's more, Rosa Stops, the development used peaceful opposition and common insubordination to focus on racial disparity, at last prompting milestone authoritative changes.

The women's activist development, which picked up speed in the late nineteenth hundred years and went on into the twentieth 100 years, looked to address orientation imbalances and secure ladies' freedoms. Floods of women's liberation have centered around issues like testimonial, regenerative privileges, work environment segregation, and orientation based viciousness, adding to critical progressions in legitimate and cultural perspectives toward orientation balance.

Natural activism has advanced because of the developing familiarity with environmental difficulties. Developments like Greenpeace, framed in the mid 1970s, have been instrumental in bringing issues to light about ecological issues, supporting for protection, and testing rehearses that hurt biological systems.

The LGBTQ+ privileges development has battled for the freedoms and acknowledgment of people of assorted sexual directions and orientation personalities. Starting with occasions like the Stall riots in 1969, the development has pushed for decriminalization, hostile to segregation regulations, and more extensive cultural acknowledgment.

Native freedoms developments, frequently pull in longstanding battles for land, independence, and social conservation, keep on upholding for the privileges and poise of native people groups worldwide. Developments like the Native American Development (Point) and the Zapatista Multitude of Public Freedom in Mexico feature the strength and opposition of native networks.

Key Drivers of Social Developments:

Social developments arise in light of a scope of elements that electrify people to on the whole test existing standards or power structures. A few key drivers include:

Bad form and Imbalance: Social developments frequently emerge because of seen treacheries and disparities inside society. Whether established in racial separation, orientation based abuse, financial abberations, or different types of foul play, developments look to address foundational lopsided characteristics.

Motivation from Past Developments: The triumphs of past friendly developments act as motivation and inspiration for current activists. Accomplishments, for example, the social equality development or ladies' testimonial show the potential for aggregate activity to achieve significant change.

Innovative Progressions: The approach of computerized correspondence and virtual entertainment has changed the scene of activism. Stages like Twitter, Facebook, and Instagram work with fast data spread, association of occasions, and the enhancement of minimized voices.

Globalization: Expanded interconnectedness and familiarity with worldwide issues add to the development of transnational developments. Activists can attract motivation and backing from battles different regions of the planet, cultivating a feeling of worldwide fortitude.

Generational Shifts: New ages frequently carry new points of view and needs to social developments. Youthful activists, driven by worries about environmental change, civil rights, and political responsibility, are effectively forming contemporary activism.

Emergency and Discontent: Snapshots of emergency, whether financial slumps, political disturbances, or general wellbeing crises, can act as impetuses for social developments. Discontent with existing frameworks might solidify into requests for change during seasons of commotion.

Lawful and Strategy Changes: Developments might be powered by a longing to impact or answer legitimate and strategy changes. For instance, developments upholding for LGBTQ+ privileges have frequently tried to challenge oppressive regulations and strategies.

Challenges Looked by Friendly Developments:

While social developments have accomplished critical triumphs, they additionally experience various difficulties that can hinder their advancement. A few normal difficulties include:

Constraint and Viciousness: Activists frequently face restraint from specialists, including captures, brutality, and concealment of contradiction. Dictator systems might utilize power to suppress developments saw as dangers to their power.

Co-optation: The co-optation of developments by political or corporate interests can weaken their unique objectives. This challenge is especially articulated when developments gain standard consideration, prompting endeavors to control or divert their stories.

Infighting and Divisions: Inward conflicts inside developments, coming from philosophical contrasts or vital methodologies, can debilitate aggregate endeavors. Infighting might divert from the development's objectives and impede its adequacy.

Media Accounts: Media depictions can shape public view of developments. One-sided or sensationalized inclusion might distort the objectives and activities of activists, affecting general assessment and political reactions.

Burnout and Exhaustion: Activism frequently requires supported exertion, and people engaged with developments might encounter burnout because of the close to home cost, individual penances, and the difficulties of confronting fundamental opposition.

Institutional Dormancy: Developments testing profoundly dug in frameworks might experience opposition from institutional designs that are impervious to change. Administrative obstacles and institutional idleness can slow advance.

Absence of Clear Administration: A few developments, deliberately or because of their decentralized nature, need clear initiative designs. While this can cultivate inclusivity, it might likewise present difficulties as far as navigation and key course.

Contemporary Activism and Developing Systems:

In the 21st hundred years, activism has developed because of the changing elements of society and correspondence. The computerized age has changed the scene of activism, giving new instruments and stages to sorting out, activating, and intensifying voices. Virtual entertainment, specifically, plays had a focal impact in working with quick correspondence, worldwide fortitude, and the spread of data.

Contemporary activism frequently accentuates inclusivity, multifacetedness, and the acknowledgment of assorted voices and encounters. Developments are progressively interconnected, with activists drawing motivation and illustrations from different causes. The People of color Matter development, for instance, interfaces with developments for racial equity around the world, perceiving the interconnected battles against foundational prejudice.

Notwithstanding customary types of dissent, contemporary activism consolidates inventive and creative procedures. Imaginative articulation, road craftsmanship, execution, and computerized crusades are utilized to pass on messages, draw in more extensive crowds, and challenge cultural standards. Activists influence the force of narrating and individual accounts to acculturate their causes and encourage sympathy.

Besides, ecological activism has acquired conspicuousness with a developing consciousness of environmental change and natural debasement. Developments like Fridays for Future, started by Greta Thunberg, have activated youthful activists internationally, calling for pressing activity to address the environment emergency. The crossing point of ecological equity with more extensive civil rights issues is a sign of contemporary activism.

Innovative headways, while giving new roads to activism, additionally present difficulties. The fast spread of deception, online badgering, and the potential for observation present dangers to activists. Cyberactivism, hacktivism, and the utilization of online stages for sorting out fights bring up moral and legitimate issues that activists should explore.

The Coronavirus pandemic has additionally reshaped activism, adjusting the elements of public social events and actual fights. Activists have adjusted by using virtual stages, online missions, and imaginative types of advanced activism to keep up with force and draw in allies.

5.1 Social Unrest and Political Activism

Social agitation and political activism are dynamic powers that shape the forms of social orders, impact political scenes, and catalyze extraordinary change. Established in discontent, disparity, and a craving for equity, social distress frequently appears as mass fights, exhibitions, and developments that challenge laid out standards and power structures. Political activism, a proactive commitment with political cycles, tries to address complaints, advocate for strategy changes, and advance civil rights. This investigation digs into the interconnected domains of social turmoil and political activism, inspecting their verifiable setting, key drivers, signs, challenges, and the advancing scene of contemporary developments.

Verifiable Setting:

The embroidery of mankind's set of experiences is woven with occasions of social agitation and political activism, mirroring the enduring battles for equity, equity, and basic freedoms. Across ages and landmasses, individuals have ascended in aggregate dispute against harsh systems, oppressive strategies, and social disparities. Authentic achievements include:

Social equality Development (1950s-1960s): The Social equality Development in the US remains as a turning point in the battle against racial isolation and segregation. Driven by figures like Martin Luther Lord Jr., Rosa Parks, and Malcolm X, the development utilized peaceful obstruction, common noncompliance, and vital activism to challenge fundamental bigotry and promoter for equivalent privileges.

Hostile to Politically-sanctioned racial segregation Development (twentieth Hundred years): The counter politically-sanctioned racial segregation development in South Africa, traversing a very long while, looked to destroy the standardized arrangement of racial isolation and separation. Activists like Nelson Mandela and associations like the African Public Congress (ANC) assumed critical parts in testing politically-sanctioned racial segregation strategies and supporting for a vote based and comprehensive South Africa.

Understudy Fights of 1968: The year 1968 saw a rush of understudy fights and social turmoil across the globe. From the US to Europe and Latin America, understudies prepared against apparent treacheries, tyranny, and issues, for example, the Vietnam War. The fights mirrored a more extensive discontent with laid out standards and power structures.

Middle Easterner Spring (2010-2012): The Bedouin Spring, a progression of favorable to a vote based system uprisings across the Middle Easterner world, denoted a huge section in contemporary political activism. Started by elements like political suppression, monetary imbalance, and debasement, the developments looked for popularity based changes and civil rights. While the results changed across nations, the Middle Easterner Spring reshaped political scenes in the area.

These verifiable examples delineate the assorted inspirations, procedures, and results of social distress and political activism. Developments have been instrumental in testing severe frameworks, getting common freedoms, and encouraging cultural changes that reverberate across ages.

Key Drivers of Social Turmoil and Political Activism:

The development of social distress and political activism is in many cases catalyzed by a conversion of elements that fuel discontent and a longing for change. A few key drivers include:

Imbalance and Foul play: Diligent financial inconsistencies, regulated segregation, and saw treacheries act as powerful impetuses for social turmoil. Developments frequently emerge because of foundational disparities that effect minimized networks.

Political Suppression: Tyrant systems, restriction, and political constraint can set off developments as individuals prepare against harsh administration. Calls for political opportunities, common freedoms, and majority rule changes become mobilizing focuses for activists.

Monetary Difficulty: Financial slumps, gravity measures, and variations in abundance conveyance can prompt boundless discontent. Developments might advocate for financial equity, laborers' freedoms, and impartial admittance to assets.

Political Debasement: Defilement inside political establishments and frameworks frequently prompts activism. Developments look to uncover and challenge degenerate works on, supporting for straightforwardness, responsibility, and great administration.

Social and Social Movements: Developing cultural standards and social movements can add to developments testing obsolete or unfair practices. Issues, for example, LGBTQ+ freedoms, orientation balance, and racial equity become central focuses for activism.

Innovative Headways: The advanced age has changed the scene of political activism. Virtual entertainment stages give spaces to quick correspondence, association, and the intensification of voices, empowering developments to pick up perceivability and speed.

Worldwide Fortitude: Consciousness of worldwide issues and the interconnectedness of battles across borders add to the development of developments with a worldwide viewpoint. Activists draw motivation from and loan backing to causes past their nearby settings.

Natural Worries: The rising consciousness of ecological corruption and environmental change has ignited another influx of activism. Developments advocate for supportable practices, environment equity, and horrendous act to address natural emergencies.

Signs of Social Distress and Political Activism:

Social turmoil and political activism take different structures, adjusting to the particular setting, main things in need of attention, and the systems utilized by activists. A few indications include:

Mass Fights and Exhibits: Huge scope fights and shows are apparent articulations of discontent and aggregate activism. From walks to assemblies, these occasions unite individuals to voice their interests and supporter for change.

Common Defiance: Common noncompliance includes peaceful protection from unreasonable regulations or arrangements. Activists might participate in demonstrations of resistance, for example, protests, strikes, or refusal to agree with specific guidelines, to cause to notice their objective.

Online Activism: The advanced age has brought about web-based activism, where people utilize virtual entertainment stages, hashtags, and computerized missions to bring issues to light, activate support, and intensify their messages. Online activism plays had a significant impact in contemporary developments.

Direct Activity: Direct activity envelops a scope of exercises focused on straightforwardly resolving issues or testing power structures. This can incorporate occupations, bars, and different types of activism that try to upset the norm and point out unambiguous complaints.

Backing and Campaigning: Activists participate in promotion and campaigning to impact policymakers and achieve regulative changes. This includes key endeavors to speak with administrators, fabricate unions, and shape public strategy.

Imaginative Articulation: Craftsmanship and culture assume a huge part in activism. Imaginative articulations like music, writing, visual expressions, and execution are utilized to pass on messages, bring out feelings, and rouse activity.

Local area Coordinating: Grassroots getting sorted out includes assembling networks at the neighborhood level. Local area coordinators work to fabricate aggregate power, address explicit issues, and enable people to become problem solvers inside their networks.

Worldwide Developments: Developments with worldwide reach, for example, the People of color Matter development and environment activism drove by figures like Greta Thunberg, epitomize the interconnected idea of contemporary activism. These developments rise above public lines, causing to notice shared worldwide difficulties.

Challenges Looked by Friendly Agitation and Political Activism:

In spite of their effect, social distress and political activism experience a scope of difficulties that can obstruct their viability. A few normal difficulties include:

Constraint and Viciousness: Activists frequently face restraint, savagery, and terrorizing from specialists or contradicting powers. State-supported brutality, captures, and crackdowns can present huge dangers to those participated in activism.

Media Outlining: The outlining of developments by media can impact public discernment. One-sided or sensationalized inclusion might distort activists' objectives, eclipsing the underlying problems and adding to public misconception.

Co-optation: The co-optation of developments by political or corporate interests can weaken their unique objectives. Developments that gain standard consideration might confront endeavors to control or divert their stories.

Infighting and Divisions: Inside conflicts inside developments, coming from philosophical contrasts or vital methodologies, can debilitate aggregate endeavors. Infighting might divert from the development's objectives and ruin its adequacy.

Burnout and Exhaustion: Activism frequently requires supported exertion, and people associated with developments might encounter burnout because of the profound cost, individual penances, and the difficulties of confronting foundational obstruction.

Absence of Clear Authority: A few developments, purposefully or because of their decentralized nature, need clear initiative designs. While this can encourage inclusivity, it might likewise present difficulties as far as navigation and vital course.

Reconnaissance and Protection Concerns: Activists might confront observation and security concerns, particularly in the advanced age. State or corporate observation can chillingly affect free articulation and the readiness of people to take part in activism.

Contemporary Scene of Activism:

In the contemporary scene, activism keeps on developing, formed by mechanical headways, worldwide interconnectedness, and the dire difficulties confronting social orders. A few prominent patterns include:

Advanced Activism: The job of computerized stages in activism has become progressively noticeable. Online entertainment works with quick correspondence, assembly, and the dispersal of data. Online activism plays had a vital impact in developments, for example, the Bedouin Spring, Possess Money Road, and People of color Matter.

Youth-Drove Developments: Youthful activists have arisen as strong problem solvers. Developments like Fridays for Future, started by Greta Thunberg, and the adolescent drove activism against firearm brutality in the US represent the effect of youth voices in molding political talk.

Interconnected Developments: Developments progressively perceive the interconnected idea of civil rights issues. Activists team up across causes, perceiving the interconnection of battles connected with race, orientation, class, and the climate.

Artivism: The combination of workmanship and activism, known as artivism, has gotten forward movement. Specialists utilize different mediums to pass on strong messages, challenge standards, and motivate activity. Creative articulation fills in as a device for drawing in different crowds and summoning close to home reactions.

Worldwide Fortitude: Activists draw motivation and backing from worldwide developments. Fortitude across borders has turned into a characterizing element of contemporary activism, with developments resounding internationally and impacting each other's methodologies.

Environment Activism: The earnestness of tending to environmental change has prodded a flood of environment activism. Developments like Termination Resistance and Dawn Development advocate for strong environment activity, natural equity, and manageability.

Wellbeing and Civil rights: The Coronavirus pandemic has featured the convergences of wellbeing and civil rights. Activists address issues like medical services inconsistencies, laborers' privileges, and the lopsided effect of the pandemic on underestimated networks.

5.2 Emerging Social Movements

Arising social developments address the advancing elements of aggregate activity, activism, and cultural change because of contemporary difficulties. These developments emerge with regards to moving social, political, and social scenes, energized by complaints, goals for equity, and a craving for fundamental change. The development of these developments mirrors the flexibility of human organization in resolving issues going from imbalance and common liberties to ecological manageability and mechanical administration. This investigation digs into the qualities, drivers, and signs of arising social developments, analyzing how they shape the account of progress in the 21st hundred years.

Qualities of Arising Social Developments:

Decentralization and Arranged Activism: Arising social developments frequently show decentralized structures, depending on organizations of activists associated through computerized stages. Not at all like various leveled associations, these developments influence the force of even correspondence, taking into account more prominent inclusivity, adaptability, and flexibility. Web-based entertainment stages assume a critical part in working with organized activism, empowering fast data scattering and preparation.

Diversity: Many arising social developments embrace a multifaceted methodology, perceiving the interconnected idea of social, monetary, and policy driven issues. This viewpoint recognizes that people might encounter different types of mistreatment in light of elements like race, orientation, class, sexuality, and the sky is the limit from there. By tending to the crossing points of personality and mistreatment, developments take a stab at a more comprehensive and all encompassing comprehension of civil rights.

Youth-Drove Activism: A critical trait of arising social developments is the noticeable quality of youth-drove activism. Youthful activists, driven by a need to get going and a longing for a superior future, play played significant parts in developments like Fridays for Future, supporting for environment activity, and the Walk for Our Lives, tending to weapon viciousness. The advanced period engages youthful activists to prepare, enhance their voices, and challenge laid out standards.

Mechanical Joining: Innovation is a focal element of arising social developments. Activists influence advanced apparatuses, virtual entertainment, and online stages to arrange, convey, and bring issues to light. Innovation works with fast preparation as well as gives a way to recording and dispersing data about treacheries, enhancing the effect of developments on a worldwide scale.

Worldwide Fortitude: Arising social developments frequently rise above public lines, cultivating a feeling of worldwide fortitude. Activists associate with similar people and developments around the world, perceiving shared battles and intensifying their aggregate effect. The interconnectedness worked with by computerized correspondence adds to the development of a worldwide dissident local area.

Imaginative Articulation and Artivism: Creative articulation, or artivism, is an unmistakable component of many arising social developments. Innovativeness, including visual expressions, music, execution, and computerized media, turns into a useful asset for passing on messages, summoning feelings, and testing cultural standards. Imaginative components improve the perceivability and reverberation of developments, connecting with different crowds.

Drivers of Arising Social Developments:

Environment Emergency and Ecological Activism: The criticalness of tending to environmental change has catalyzed the development of natural activism. Developments like Annihilation Disobedience and Dawn Development advocate for intense environment activity, natural equity, and maintainability. Activists request foundational changes to moderate the effect of human exercises in the world and advance environmental supportability.

Mechanical Administration and Computerized Freedoms: The rising impact of innovation in administration and day to day existence has led to developments zeroed in on advanced privileges and mechanical administration. Worries about observation, protection encroachments, and the moral ramifications of arising advancements have prompted developments upholding for straightforward and responsible innovation approaches.

Racial Equity Developments: The resurgence of developments pushing for racial equity, for example, People of color Matter, has picked up speed in light of cases of police ruthlessness and foundational prejudice. These developments challenge primary disparities, call for police change, and backer for the destroying of bigoted frameworks.

Women's activist and LGBTQ+ Developments: Continuous battles for orientation fairness, regenerative freedoms, and LGBTQ+ privileges keep on molding arising social developments. Activists challenge man centric standards, advocate for inclusivity, and take a stab at lawful and social acknowledgment of different orientation characters and sexual directions.

Wellbeing Value Developments: The worldwide Coronavirus pandemic has carried issues of wellbeing value to the very front. Developments zeroing in on fair admittance to medical services, antibody appropriation, and tending to fundamental wellbeing differences have acquired unmistakable quality, underscoring the interconnectedness of wellbeing and civil rights.

Monetary Equity and Work Developments: Financial imbalances and worries about specialists' privileges have energized arising social developments supporting for monetary equity. Developments, for example, Battle for $15 call for fair wages, further developed work conditions, and a more evenhanded dispersion of riches.

A vote based system and Common liberties Developments: Developments pushing for a majority rule government, common liberties, and political opportunities are pervasive in settings where despotism, restriction, and dictatorship present difficulties. Activists make progress toward comprehensive administration, security of common freedoms, and the maintaining of majority rule standards.

Signs of Arising Social Developments:

Worldwide Environment Strikes: Drove by youth activists like Greta Thunberg, worldwide environment strikes have become symbolic of the ecological activism related with arising social developments. Youth-drove developments, like Fridays for Future, arrange huge scope strikes and fights to request earnest environment activity and strategy changes.

#BlackLivesMatter Development: The #BlackLivesMatter development, ignited by occurrences of police mercilessness against Dark people, has turned into a worldwide call for racial equity. Activists utilize virtual entertainment, fights, and support to challenge foundational prejudice, advance police change, and advance the reason for racial equity.

#MeToo Development: The #MeToo development, starting from survivors' accounts of lewd behavior and attack, has revealed insight into the commonness of such encounters. The development advocates for a finish to working environment badgering, changes in social mentalities toward orientation based brutality, and expanded responsibility for culprits.

Termination Defiance: Eradication Resistance (XR) is a worldwide natural development known for its polite insubordination and guide activity to draw focus toward the environment emergency. XR activists take part in peaceful fights, disturbances, and demonstrations of common rebellion to request pressing government activity on environmental change.

Computerized Freedoms Support: Developments upholding for advanced privileges center around issues like internet based security, information assurance, and fighting reconnaissance. Associations like the Electronic Wilderness Establishment (EFF) work to safeguard common freedoms in the advanced age and guarantee that innovation serves the interests of people as opposed to severe foundations.

Worldwide Wellbeing Value Activism: The Coronavirus pandemic has prodded developments pushing for worldwide wellbeing value. Activists accentuate the requirement for fair immunization appropriation, available medical care, and resolving fundamental issues that add to wellbeing variations inside and between countries.

Hostile to Algorithmic Inclination Activism: As worries about algorithmic predisposition and oppressive advances develop, developments arise to resolve these issues. Activists and associations work to feature and challenge predispositions implanted in calculations that can sustain social disparities, particularly in regions like law enforcement and recruiting.

Challenges Looked by Arising Social Developments:

Co-optation and Weakening: Arising social developments face the gamble of co-optation, where their objectives might be weakened or diverted by political or corporate interests. The mainstreaming of developments can prompt a deficiency of spotlight on foundational issues and a diluting of their unique requests.

State Constraint and Brutality: Activists in arising social developments frequently experience state restraint, viciousness, and terrorizing. States might send strategies like captures, restriction, and utilization of power to smother contradict, presenting huge difficulties to the maintainability and effect of developments.

Online Provocation and Disinformation: The computerized idea of arising social developments opens activists to online badgering, disinformation crusades, and cyber-attacks. Malignant entertainers might try to subvert developments by spreading bogus data, focusing on activists, and establishing a threatening internet based climate.

Burnout and Dissident Weakness: Supported activism can prompt burnout and weariness among activists. The profound cost, the consistent requirement for backing, and the difficulties of exploring complex issues add to the gamble of extremist burnout, influencing the congruity and adequacy of developments.

Inward Divisions: Arising social developments, especially those with decentralized structures, may encounter interior divisions. Conflicts over methodologies, objectives, or philosophical contrasts can ruin strong activity and debilitate the general effect of the development.

Media Stories and Outlining: Media accounts assume a pivotal part in molding public view of developments. One-sided or sensationalized inclusion can twist the targets and messages of activists, possibly prompting public misconception and an absence of help.

Absence of Foundational Change: Notwithstanding causing to notice explicit issues, arising social developments might confront difficulties in accomplishing considerable fundamental change. Now and again, developments might get representative triumphs without tending to the underlying drivers of the issues they try to change.

Future Directions of Arising Social Developments:

Proceeded with Diversity: The multifaceted methodology, perceiving the interconnected idea of different types of mistreatment, is probably going to keep molding arising social developments. Developments that address covering issues connected with race, orientation, financial equity, and the climate might acquire unmistakable quality.

Imaginative Types of Activism: The advanced age will probably observe the development of creative types of activism. Computer generated reality, decentralized advances, and new correspondence stages might furnish activists with novel apparatuses for arranging, activating, and drawing in more extensive crowds.

Expanded Joint effort: Arising social developments may progressively team up across topographical and issue-based limits. Worldwide fortitude and shared methodologies might turn out to be more pervasive as activists perceive the force of aggregate activity in tending to mind boggling, interconnected difficulties.

Accentuation on Foundational Arrangements: Developments are probably going to underscore the requirement for fundamental arrangements instead of shallow or representative changes. Activists might push for authoritative changes, strategy changes, and institutional changes to address the underlying drivers of social issues.

Computerized Strength: With the continuous difficulties of online badgering and disinformation, arising social developments might foster procedures for advanced versatility. This could include taking on secure specialized devices, building on the web networks impervious to control, and teaching activists about internet based dangers.

Youth Strengthening: The young drove nature of many arising social developments is supposed to continue. As more youthful ages keep on participating in activism, their viewpoints, values, and imaginative methodologies might shape the direction of developments and impact cultural standards.

Developing Extremist Stories: Dissident accounts might advance to incorporate a more extensive comprehension of equity, value, and basic freedoms. Developments may progressively zero in on building comprehensive stories that reverberate with assorted crowds and challenge existing power structures.

5.3 Governments' Response to Social Change

Legislatures assume a crucial part in molding the reaction to social change, as they explore the complicated elements of developing cultural requirements, goals, and requests. The connection among state run administrations and social change is complex, including strategy detailing, execution, and variation to address arising difficulties. This investigation dives into the multi-layered manners by which state run administrations answer social change, analyzing the systems, difficulties, and suggestions innate in their communications with developing cultural elements.

Strategy Definition and Execution:

Legislatures answer social change basically through the plan and execution of approaches. Approaches act as the administrative system through which states address major problems, enact cultural standards, and distribute assets. The arrangement making process includes recognizing difficulties, counseling partners, drafting regulation, and, critically, guaranteeing implementation.

Transformation to Social Movements: Cultural qualities and social standards go through consistent development. Legislatures, perceiving the powerful idea of culture, frequently change approaches to line up with changing cultural assumptions. This might include changes in regions like schooling, family regulation, and social portrayal to think about advancing points of view variety, inclusivity, and civil rights.

Financial Arrangements In light of Imbalance: Social change frequently focuses on monetary variations and the requirement for fair dissemination of assets. State run administrations might answer by forming financial approaches pointed toward lessening pay disparity, further developing admittance to schooling and medical services, and executing social government assistance programs. The objective is to address the underlying drivers of social issues connected with monetary divergence.

Regulation for Basic freedoms and Common Freedoms: As social orders progress, there is an increased familiarity with basic liberties and common freedoms. Legislatures answer calls for equity and equity by sanctioning or correcting regulation to safeguard individual privileges. This incorporates resolving issues, for example, orientation equity, LGBTQ+ freedoms, and racial equity, guaranteeing that lawful structures line up with advancing cultural standards.

Challenges in Strategy Reaction:

While state run administrations expect to address social change through approach, they face various difficulties that can block successful reactions. These difficulties emerge from the intricacies of cultural issues, political elements, and the assorted necessities of the populace.

Strategy Idleness: Regulatory dormancy and protection from change inside government designs can thwart quick reactions to social change. Laid out foundations might be hesitant to adjust or may confront deterrents in carrying out new approaches, dialing back the most common way of resolving major problems.

Political Polarization: Political polarization can discourage the agreement expected to sanction significant arrangements. Divisions among ideological groups or philosophical contrasts inside overseeing bodies might bring about gridlock, making it trying to pass regulation that actually resolves social issues.

Momentary Political Contemplations: Legislatures, particularly those confronting normal races, may focus on transient political contemplations over long haul cultural advantages. This can prompt approach choices driven by discretionary cycles instead of supported endeavors to address fundamental social difficulties.

Obstruction from Vested parties: Strong vested parties, addressing explicit areas or belief systems, may oppose strategy changes that rock the boat. Campaigning endeavors, crusade commitments, and backing can impact policymakers and discourage changes that contradict personal stakes.

Absence of Public Help or Mindfulness: Fruitful arrangement execution frequently depends on open help and mindfulness. States might battle to resolve social issues assuming that there is deficient comprehension or public support for proposed arrangements. Viable correspondence and public commitment become basic in exploring this test.

Worldwide Interconnectedness: In a time of worldwide interconnectedness, states might find it trying to answer social change in detachment. Issues, for example, environmental change, pandemics, and relocation require cooperative, worldwide endeavors. Public reactions might be deficient without collaboration on a worldwide scale.

Social Projects and Government assistance Drives:

States answer social change by establishing social projects and government assistance drives intended to address explicit requirements inside the populace. These drives intend to offer help, lighten difficulties, and upgrade the general prosperity of residents.

Neediness Mitigation Projects: States carry out destitution easing projects to address financial differences. These projects might incorporate money move plans, food help, and occupation creation drives pointed toward lifting weak populaces out of destitution.

Training Changes: Perceiving the extraordinary force of schooling, legislatures frequently answer social change by executing changes in the training area. This might include changes in educational program to reflect contemporary qualities, endeavors to improve admittance to schooling, and drives to address abberations in instructive results.

Medical services Openness: Social change frequently highlights the significance of medical care availability. Legislatures answer by extending medical care administrations, further developing framework, and carrying out general wellbeing drives. Reactions might be especially articulated during wellbeing emergencies, like pandemics, where states assume an essential part in overseeing and moderating the effect.

Social Lodging and Metropolitan Turn of events: because of changing socio-economics and urbanization, states might put resources into social lodging and metropolitan improvement projects. These drives mean to give reasonable lodging choices, work on everyday environments, and establish supportable metropolitan conditions.

Challenges in Carrying out Friendly Projects:

While social projects are fundamental for tending to social change, legislatures experience difficulties in their plan, subsidizing, and execution. Conquering these difficulties is significant for the viability and manageability of such drives.

Asset Limitations: Sufficient subsidizing is fundamental for the outcome of social projects. States might confront asset imperatives, contending monetary needs, or financial slumps that limit their ability to assign adequate assets to social drives.

Managerial Effectiveness: The proficient organization of social projects is basic for their prosperity. Regulatory shortcomings, defilement, and absence of straight-forwardness can obstruct the powerful execution of projects, frustrating their effect on the planned recipients.

Observing and Assessment: Continuous checking and assessment are important to survey the effect of social projects. Legislatures might confront difficulties in laying out vigorous checking systems, prompting troubles in measuring the adequacy of drives and making fundamental changes.

Focusing on Weak Populaces: Guaranteeing that social projects arrive at the planned recipients, especially weak populaces, requires exact focusing on. Legislatures might experience difficulties in distinguishing and arriving at those out of luck, prompting possible holes in the conveyance of administrations.

Political Obstruction: Social projects can be defenseless to political impedance, with state run administrations involving them for political addition as opposed to tending to authentic social necessities. This can bring about the misallocation of assets and a mutilation of program goals.

Lawful and Administrative Structures:

Legislatures answer social change by adjusting or making lawful and administrative structures that reflect developing cultural qualities. This includes refreshing existing regulations, presenting new regulation, and laying out administrative bodies to resolve arising issues.

Social liberties Regulation: States answer calls for equity and fairness by sanctioning or altering social equality regulation. This incorporates regulations that shield people from segregation in view of race, orientation, religion, sexual direction, and different qualities. Legitimate systems advance to line up with changing cultural standards and assumptions.

Natural Guidelines: The acknowledgment of ecological worries prompts legislatures to lay out or upgrade natural guidelines. These guidelines plan to moderate the effect of human exercises on the climate, address environmental change, and advance manageable practices across enterprises.

Advanced and Security Regulations: The multiplication of innovation has driven legislatures to answer with regulation tending to computerized privileges and protection. Legislatures lay out regulations that control the assortment and utilization of individual information, battle cybercrime, and guarantee the security of people in the computerized circle.

Work Regulations: Social change frequently prompts amendments to work regulations to resolve issues like specialists' privileges, fair wages, and working environment wellbeing. State run administrations might adjust work guidelines to line up with developing business rehearses and the changing idea of work.

Challenges in Lawful and Administrative Reactions:

While lawful and administrative structures are fundamental for answering social change, legislatures experience difficulties in their turn of events, authorization, and transformation.

Regulative Slack: The official interaction can be slow, prompting a slack between the recognizable proof of social issues and the order of significant regulations. Regulative bodies might battle to stay up with the speed of cultural change, bringing about obsolete or deficient lawful structures.

Requirement Difficulties: Even with vigorous legitimate systems, compelling authorization is urgent. State run administrations might confront difficulties in guaranteeing consistence, especially in situations where there is opposition from personal stakes or when administrative bodies miss the mark on assets for thorough authorization.

Unseen side-effects: Changes to lawful and administrative structures can have potentially negative results. States should cautiously consider the possible effects of new regulations to abstain from compounding existing issues or making new difficulties.

Globalization and Harmonization: In an interconnected world, legislatures might experience difficulties in orchestrating legitimate structures with global guidelines. Offsetting public interests with worldwide assumptions requires vital discretion and discussion.

Flexibility to Arising Innovations: The quick speed of mechanical progression presents difficulties for administrative structures. Legislatures might battle to adjust existing regulations to address arising advancements, prompting holes in guideline and expected dangers to cultural prosperity.

Public Commitment and Participatory Administration:

State run administrations progressively perceive the significance of public commitment and participatory administration as necessary parts of answering social change. Comprehensive dynamic cycles that include residents, common society associations, and partners add to additional responsive and supportable arrangements.

Meeting and Exchange: States participate in conference and discourse with residents to grasp their interests, goals, and viewpoints. This participatory methodology guarantees that strategies are educated by a different reach regarding voices, improving their pertinence and acknowledgment.

Local area Based Direction: because of confined social change, legislatures might take on local area based dynamic cycles. This includes enabling networks to partake in choices that straightforwardly influence them, encouraging a feeling of pride and collaboration.

Resident Criticism Components: Laying out criticism instruments permits residents to give input on government arrangements and projects. States might use overviews, public discussions, and computerized stages to assemble criticism and check public feeling.

Challenges in Open Commitment:

While public commitment is significant for successful administration, legislatures experience difficulties in cultivating significant support and conquering hindrances to resident association.

Inclusivity and Portrayal: Guaranteeing inclusivity and portrayal in participatory cycles is testing. A few gatherings, particularly underestimated or underrepresented networks, may confront boundaries to investment. State run administrations should effectively address these abberations to abstain from supporting existing imbalances.

Data Deviation: Resident cooperation is dependent upon admittance to exact and exhaustive data. States might battle with data lopsidedness, where certain gatherings miss the mark on vital information or assets to connect definitively in dynamic cycles.

Hypocrisy and Emblematic Cooperation: There is a gamble of posturing and representative support, where states draw in residents in a shallow way without really integrating their contribution to direction. Guaranteeing that participatory cycles are considerable and effective requires proactive endeavors to keep away from tokenistic approaches.

Limit Building: Building the limit of residents and networks to effectively take part in administration processes is a test. Legislatures might have to put resources into schooling and preparing projects to engage people with the abilities required for successful commitment.

Overseeing Clashing Perspectives: Public commitment frequently includes overseeing assorted and in some cases clashing perspectives. States should explore these distinctions carefully, cultivating a climate where useful exchange can occur without plunging into disunity.

Worldwide Collaboration and Strategy:

Given the interconnected idea of worldwide difficulties, state run administrations answer social change through global collaboration and strategy. Cooperative endeavors permit countries to address shared concerns, for example, environmental change, general wellbeing emergencies, and relocation.

Environment Arrangements: Legislatures take part in worldwide environment arrangements to address ecological difficulties aggregately. Arrangements like the Paris Understanding expect to join countries chasing supportable practices, emanation decreases, and environment versatility.

Worldwide Wellbeing Drives: Answering pandemics and wellbeing emergencies frequently includes global cooperation. Legislatures draw in with worldwide associations, like the World Wellbeing Association (WHO), and take part in joint endeavors to address worldwide wellbeing challenges.

Movement Strategies and Tact: Relocation, driven by friendly, financial, and political variables, requires conciliatory reactions. Legislatures team up on relocation strategies, arrange arrangements, and participate in exchange to deal with the difficulties and potential open doors related with movement.

Exchange and Financial Collaboration: Monetary changes and social moves frequently brief states to take part in global economic accords and monetary collaboration. These drives look to encourage monetary development, set out open doors for residents, and address difficulties emerging from globalization.

Challenges in Global Collaboration:

While global collaboration is fundamental, legislatures face difficulties in adjusting assorted public interests, arranging arrangements, and defeating international strains.

Public Interest versus Worldwide Participation: Offsetting public interests with the basic for worldwide collaboration presents difficulties. States might focus on homegrown worries over worldwide joint effort, particularly when confronted with contending requests from their constituents.

International Pressures: Discretionary endeavors can be blocked by international strains and clashes. States should explore complex global relations, address authentic hostilities, and settle on something worth agreeing on to work with compelling collaboration.

Discriminatory Power Elements: Worldwide administration designs can display biased power elements, where certain countries employ lopsided impact. This can upset compelling cooperation and result in results that don't satisfactorily address the necessities of less strong countries.

Asset Allotment and Fair Weight Sharing: Worldwide collaboration frequently requires monetary and asset commitments from taking part countries. Abberations in asset designation and the weight sharing related with tending to worldwide difficulties can strain cooperative endeavors.

Multilateral versus Two-sided Approaches: States should choose multilateral and reciprocal ways to deal with worldwide collaboration. Picking the best methodology relies upon the idea of the issue, the ability of countries to team up, and the intricacy of international connections.

Chapter 6

Environmental Agenda and Sustainability

The ecological plan and supportability have arisen as focal points of support in forming worldwide strategies and cultural cognizance. As the world wrestles with the outcomes of environmental change, loss of biodiversity, and natural debasement, state run administrations, associations, and people are progressively perceiving the basic to focus on manageable practices and protection endeavors. This investigation digs into the multi-layered elements of the ecological plan, looking at the difficulties, strategy reactions, and developing ideal models chasing a feasible future.

Challenges in the Ecological Scene:

The ecological difficulties going up against the world are complex and inter-connected, traversing environmental change, biodiversity misfortune, contamination, and asset exhaustion. These moves present huge dangers to environments, human prosperity, and the general soundness of the planet.

Environmental Change: Maybe the most squeezing ecological test, environmental change is driven by human exercises, principally the consuming of petroleum products and deforestation. The subsequent expansion in ozone harming substance outflows has prompted an Earth-wide temperature boost, with outcomes, for example, rising ocean levels, outrageous climate occasions, and disturbances to environments.

Biodiversity Misfortune: The sped up loss of biodiversity is an outcome of territory obliteration, overexploitation of normal assets, contamination, and environ-mental change. This misfortune subverts the strength of environments, upsets natural equilibrium, and decreases the potential for logical, financial, and social advantages got from different biological systems.

Contamination: Contamination in different structures, including air, water, and soil contamination, presents extreme dangers to ecological and human well-being. Modern emanations, agrarian overflow, and ill-advised garbage removal add to contamination, influencing air quality, polluting water sources, and corrupting soil ripeness.

Asset Exhaustion: Unreasonable utilization examples and asset abuse lead to consumption of limited assets, including backwoods, fisheries, and minerals. Over-extraction and fumble of assets add to natural debasement and worsen social and financial inconsistencies.

Land Debasement: The corruption of arable land through cycles like deforestation, desertification, and soil disintegration sabotages agrarian efficiency and intensifies food weakness. Unreasonable land use rehearses add to the deficiency of prolific soil, affecting worldwide food frameworks.

Strategy Reactions and Peaceful accords:

States and global associations have answered the natural difficulties through the plan of strategies and arrangements pointed toward encouraging manageable turn of events, protection, and environment activity.

Paris Understanding: The Paris Arrangement, embraced in 2015, remains as a milestone global accord pointed toward moderating environmental change. The arrangement tries to restrict an unnatural weather change to well under 2 degrees Celsius above pre-modern levels and seek after endeavors to restrict the temperature increment to 1.5 degrees Celsius. Taking an interest countries focus on broadly resolved commitments (NDCs) framing their endeavors to diminish ozone depleting substance emanations.

Show on Natural Variety (CBD): The CBD, laid out in 1992, addresses the protection of organic variety and the feasible utilization of its parts. The Show accentuates the significance of keeping up with environments and biodiversity for the prosperity of present and people in the future. Progressing talks for a post-2020 worldwide biodiversity structure intend to improve endeavors to end biodiversity misfortune.

Practical Improvement Objectives (SDGs): The Unified Countries' SDGs incorporate explicit targets connected with natural supportability. Objectives, for example, "Environment Activity" (Objective 13), "Life Beneath Water" (Objective 14), and "Life Ashore" (Objective 15) highlight the interconnectedness of ecological, social, and financial aspects chasing feasible turn of events.

Round Economy Drives: Legislatures and organizations are progressively embracing the idea of a round economy, which intends to limit squander and advance the manageable utilization of assets. Drives incorporate reusing programs, the advancement of eco-accommodating items, and the plan of items for solidness and recyclability.

Sustainable power Strategies: The change to environmentally friendly power sources is a critical part of natural approaches around the world. State run administrations are taking on measures to boost the turn of events and utilization of sustainable power advancements, for example, sun based, wind, and hydropower, to diminish reliance on petroleum derivatives.

Challenges in Executing Natural Approaches:

While critical steps have been made in planning natural strategies, their compelling execution faces different difficulties established in political, monetary, and social elements.

Political Will and Responsibility: The effective execution of ecological strategies requires political will and responsibility from states. Political needs, momentary discretionary contemplations, and clashing interests might obstruct the reception and requirement of hearty ecological guidelines.

Worldwide Imbalance: Abberations in monetary turn of events and asset access between countries add to worldwide ecological difficulties. Emerging nations might confront troubles in executing severe natural approaches while tending to squeezing financial requirements, prompting difficulties in accomplishing global maintainability objectives.

Corporate Impact: The impact of strong companies with personal stakes in impractical practices represents a test to the execution of ecological strategies. Campaigning, effort commitments, and protection from administrative structures can subvert endeavors to implement naturally dependable practices.

Absence of Requirement Components: now and again, natural approaches need hearty implementation systems, permitting rebelliousness without outcomes. Feeble administrative structures and lacking checking add to difficulties in considering people and elements responsible for natural infringement.

Public Mindfulness and Commitment: The outcome of natural arrangements frequently relies on open mindfulness and commitment. Inadequate public getting it, lack of care, or protection from social changes can impede the viability of approaches pointed toward advancing manageable practices.

Nearby and Local area Drove Drives:
Perceiving the significance of neighborhood commitment, grassroots developments, and local area drove drives have acquired unmistakable quality as compelling ways to deal with tending to natural difficulties.

Local area Protection: Nearby people group frequently assume a pivotal part in preservation endeavors. Local area based drives for supportable asset the executives, reforestation, and territory reclamation engage people to take part in natural stewardship effectively.

Native Information and Practices: Native people group, with their profound association with nature, contribute significant information and practices for maintainable asset the executives. Perceiving and regarding native freedoms and consolidating conventional biological information can upgrade natural preservation endeavors.

Resident Science: Resident science drives connect with people in general in logical examination and information assortment connected with ecological issues. Resident researchers contribute important data on subjects like biodiversity, air and water quality, and environment designs, improving the comprehension of biological cycles.

Nearby Maintainability Undertakings: Neighborhood supportability projects, including local area gardens, sustainable power cooperatives, and waste decrease drives, exhibit the potential for decentralized, local area driven answers for natural difficulties.

Advancements in Maintainable Innovations:

Mechanical headways assume a vital part in molding the ecological plan by offering imaginative answers for moderate natural effect and advance economical practices.

Sustainable power Innovations: The turn of events and organization of sustainable power advancements, like sunlight based chargers, wind turbines, and high level energy stockpiling frameworks, add to the progress toward a low-carbon energy scene.

Green Framework: Green foundation drives, including green rooftops, penetrable asphalts, and metropolitan green spaces, expect to improve natural versatility in metropolitan conditions. These arrangements moderate the effects of urbanization on biological systems and add to environment variation.

Accuracy Agribusiness: Accuracy horticulture use innovation, including sensors, robots, and information examination, to streamline farming practices. This approach lessens asset inputs, limits ecological effect, and upgrades the productivity and maintainability of food creation.

Roundabout Economy Advances: Advancements that help a round economy, like reusing developments, manageable bundling arrangements, and shut circle creation processes, add to limiting waste and boosting the effective utilization of assets.

Difficulties and Contemplations in Mechanical Arrangements:

While maintainable innovations offer promising arrangements, difficulties and contemplations should be addressed to guarantee their viability and moral execution.

Innovative Access and Disparity: Admittance to maintainable advances isn't uniform internationally, prompting mechanical imbalance. Guaranteeing evenhanded admittance to advancements is critical to abstain from intensifying existing financial inconsistencies.

E-Squander and Natural Effect: The creation and removal of electronic gadgets add to electronic waste (e-squander) and natural contamination. Manageable innovation arrangements should address the existence pattern of items, taking into account asset extraction, fabricating cycles, and end-of-life removal.

Moral Ramifications: The reception of new advancements raises moral contemplations, including issues connected with protection, information security, and the possible potentially negative side-effects of development. A cautious equilibrium should be struck between mechanical advancement and moral protections.

Reliance on Innovation: Overreliance on mechanical arrangements without resolving hidden fundamental issues might bring about a shallow way to deal with natural difficulties. Supportable advancements ought to supplement more extensive endeavors to advance fundamental change and capable utilization.

Changes in Purchaser Conduct and Corporate Obligation:

Changes in purchaser conduct and corporate practices are instrumental in driving the reception of maintainable practices and affecting more extensive natural patterns.

Purchaser Mindfulness and Cognizant Utilization: Expanding mindfulness among buyers with respect to the ecological effect of their decisions has prompted a developing interest for manageable items. Cognizant utilization, set apart by inclinations for eco-accommodating choices, upholds the advancement of reasonable business sectors.

Corporate Social Obligation (CSR): Numerous organizations are perceiving the significance of incorporating ecological contemplations into their plans of action. CSR drives envelop responsibilities to diminish fossil fuel byproducts, limit ecological impression, and take part in charitable endeavors supporting natural preservation.

Green Money and Feasible Speculations: The monetary area assumes a part in advancing maintainability through green money and economical ventures. Financial backers progressively think about natural, social, and administration (ESG) factors in their direction, impacting corporate way of behaving toward additional supportable practices.

Roundabout Plans of action: A few organizations are embracing roundabout plans of action that focus on asset proficiency, reusing, and item life span. Planning items in view of recyclability and laying out reclaim programs add to the round economy.

Challenges in Moving Customer and Corporate Practices:
While positive changes in customer conduct and corporate obligation are clear, challenges continue encouraging far reaching reception of economical practices.

Greenwashing: Greenwashing, or the misleading advancement of items or practices as harmless to the ecosystem, represents a test to informed purchaser decisions. Guaranteeing straightforwardness and responsibility in corporate informing is vital to forestall misdirecting claims.

Moderateness and Openness: Supportable items and practices ought to be open and reasonable to an expansive range of purchasers. Beating boundaries connected with cost and accessibility is fundamental to democratize admittance to eco-accommodating other options.

Protection from Change: Customer propensities and corporate practices dug in ordinary models might oppose quick advances to supportability. Empowering social change and hierarchical changes requires viable correspondence, training, and motivations.

Administrative Structures and Authorization: The turn of events and requirement of administrative systems are crucial for guide and boost maintainable practices. Frail or lacking guidelines might block progress, stressing the requirement for strong lawful structures and implementation components.

The Job of Instruction and Promotion:
Training and promotion assume vital parts in forming public figuring out, encouraging ecological stewardship, and activating aggregate activity.

Natural Training: Coordinating ecological instruction into school educational programs and public mindfulness crusades improves comprehension of environmental frameworks, biodiversity, and the effect of human exercises. Training engages people to go with informed decisions and effectively take part in natural protection.

Promotion and Activism: Natural support and activism enhance public voices, consider policymakers and partnerships responsible, and drive foundational change. Grassroots developments, drove by activists and promoters, assume a basic part in bringing issues to light and preparing networks for ecological causes.

Media and Correspondence: The media fills in as a useful asset for dispersing data and molding public talk on natural issues. Dependable news-casting, narratives, and virtual entertainment stages add to building a worldwide ecological cognizance.

Challenges in Ecological Schooling and Promotion:

Notwithstanding the extraordinary capability of schooling and promotion, challenges endure in actually conveying natural issues and activating expansive based help.

Deception and Greenwashing: The multiplication of falsehood and greenwashing presents difficulties to exact ecological schooling. Basic media proficiency and truth checking abilities are fundamental for knowing tenable data from deluding stories.

Political Impedance: Ecological training and support endeavors might confront political obstruction, restriction, or endeavors to make light of the earnestness of natural issues. State run administrations and personal stakes might look to control accounts to suit their plans.

Inclusivity and Variety: Guaranteeing inclusivity and variety in natural training and support is vital. Portrayal of different voices, points of view, and encounters adds to a more thorough comprehension of natural difficulties and arrangements.

Lobbyist Burnout: Activists and supporters might confront burnout because of the close to home cost of natural issues and the difficulties related with affecting change. Building steady organizations, advancing taking care of oneself, and resolving foundational issues are fundamental for supporting backing endeavors.

6.1 Environmental Concerns in the Post-Pandemic Era

The post-pandemic period has introduced an increased familiarity with ecological worries, stressing the complex exchange between human exercises, biological system wellbeing, and worldwide manageability.

As the world wrestles with the repercussions of the Coronavirus pandemic, there is a developing acknowledgment that natural contemplations are necessary to building strong and fair social orders. This investigation dives into the ecological worries that have come to the front in the post-pandemic time, analyzing the convergences of general wellbeing, biodiversity, environmental change, and the basic for feasible practices.

General Wellbeing and Ecological Association:

The Coronavirus pandemic has highlighted the mind boggling connection between general wellbeing and the climate. Zoonotic sicknesses, those communicated among creatures and people, feature the weaknesses emerging from infringements into normal living spaces, untamed life exchange, and the strengthening of horticulture.

Zoonotic Transmission and Biodiversity Misfortune: The infringement into normal biological systems, frequently determined by deforestation and urbanization, carries people into nearer contact with natural life. This builds the gamble of zoonotic transmission of infections, as shown by the starting points of the SARS-CoV-2 infection. Biodiversity misfortune further worsens this gamble, as decreased species variety might prompt the expansion of specific host species that can convey illnesses.

Biological system Wellbeing and Strength: Solid environments go about as cushions against the development and spread of infections. Biodiverse conditions will more often than not regulatorily affect sickness vectors, restricting their multiplication. The debasement of biological systems, in any case, compromises this normal guard component, leaving populaces more powerless to novel microorganisms.

Metropolitan Preparation and General Wellbeing: The plan of metropolitan spaces impacts general wellbeing results. Post-pandemic metropolitan arranging underscores the significance of green spaces, supportable framework, and tough city formats. Admittance to nature inside metropolitan conditions upholds mental prosperity as well as adds to illness moderation by encouraging biodiversity and lessening stressors that can think twice about resistant framework.

Environmental Change Alleviation and Variation:
As social orders recuperate from the pandemic, there is a reestablished center around tending to the approaching danger of environmental change. The basic to change to low-carbon economies and construct environment strength has acquired conspicuousness in post-pandemic recuperation procedures.

Green Recuperation and Supportable Ventures: Numerous state run administrations are incorporating natural contemplations into their recuperation plans, adjusting financial improvement measures with environment activity. Interests in environmentally friendly power, feasible framework, and nature-based arrangements add to both financial recuperation and long haul environment versatility.

Environment Related Wellbeing Dangers: Environmental change presents immediate and backhanded dangers to general wellbeing. Climbing temperatures, outrageous climate occasions, and changing illness designs influence networks around the world. The post-pandemic time requires a comprehensive methodology that considers environmental change relief as a basic part of protecting general wellbeing.

Weakness and Value: The effects of environmental change excessively influence weak populaces, worsening existing disparities. The post-pandemic reaction accentuates the requirement for impartial environment strategies that address the weaknesses of underestimated networks, perceiving that versatility building measures should be comprehensive and socially.

Feasible Practices and Round Economy:
The interruptions brought about by the pandemic have incited a reconsideration of utilization designs and a revitalized obligation to supportable practices. The idea of a roundabout economy, where assets are reused, reused, and reused, is building up forward momentum as a way to limit squander and diminish ecological effect.

Single-Use Plastics and Waste Decrease: The flood in single-use plastics during the pandemic, driven by worries over cleanliness, has featured the ecological outcomes of expendable items. Post-pandemic, there is a push for squander decrease systems, including the advancement of reusable other options and the execution of strategies to control single-use plastics.

Restricted and Manageable Stockpile Chains: The pandemic uncovered weaknesses in worldwide stock chains, provoking a shift towards limited and versatile stock organizations. Reasonable obtaining, moral creation rehearses, and decreased reliance on significant distance transportation are key contemplations in building more practical and strong stock chains.

Sustainable power Change: The basic to diminish reliance on petroleum derivatives has picked up speed in the post-pandemic time. Interests in sustainable power sources, energy proficiency measures, and the getting rid of petroleum product appropriations are necessary to both monetary recuperation and natural maintainability.

Nature-Based Arrangements and Protection:

The acknowledgment of nature-based arrangements as basic parts of post-pandemic recuperation mirrors a comprehension of the significant commitments of solid environments to human prosperity.

Green Framework and Biodiversity Protection: Green foundation, which incorporates parks, woods, and metropolitan green spaces, adds to biodiversity preservation and gives fundamental biological system administrations. Post-pandemic recuperation plans underline the creation and conservation of such spaces to upgrade versatility, work on psychological wellness, and backing biodiversity.

Eco-The travel industry and Manageable Practices: The travel industry area, frequently hard-hit by the pandemic, is going through a change towards additional feasible practices. Eco-the travel industry drives that focus on protection, local area commitment, and low-influence the travel industry are acquiring noticeable quality as nations look to resuscitate their travel industry businesses in naturally capable ways.

Safeguarded Regions and Rebuilding Undertakings: The foundation of safeguarded regions and reclamation projects is necessary to biodiversity protection. Post-pandemic recuperation techniques incorporate drives to extend safeguarded regions, reestablish corrupted environments, and improve biodiversity hallways to work with the development of species.

Challenges in the Post-Pandemic Natural Plan:

While there is a developing agreement on the requirement for ecological contemplations in post-pandemic recuperation, a few difficulties prevent the successful execution of supportable practices.

Transient Monetary Tensions: Legislatures and organizations face the test of adjusting momentary financial tensions with long haul maintainability objectives. The direness to recuperate from the monetary slump might prompt choices that focus on quick acquires over feasible practices.

Strategy Execution and Requirement: The improvement of maintainable arrangements is only the initial step; viable execution and authorization are significant. Conflicting implementation, absence of administrative instruments, and opposition from personal stakes present difficulties to the effective execution of natural strategies.

Worldwide Collaboration and Administration: Numerous ecological difficulties, for example, environmental change and biodiversity misfortune, require worldwide participation. The post-pandemic time exposes the requirement for reinforced worldwide administration structures and cooperative endeavors to address transboundary ecological issues.

Public Mindfulness and Conduct Change: Moving cultural way of behaving towards maintainability requires powerful open mindfulness crusades and instructive drives. Defeating imbued utilization examples and cultivating a feeling of natural stewardship require supported endeavors in training and promotion.

Mechanical Development and Access: The arrangement of maintainable innovations is fundamental to natural objectives. In any case, guaranteeing fair admittance to these advances and addressing the computerized partition are moves that should be addressed to forestall the compounding of existing financial differences.

6.2 Political Commitments to Sustainability

Political responsibilities to supportability have become progressively focal in worldwide talk as countries wrestle with the pressing need to address natural difficulties, advance social value, and guarantee financial strength. The complicated interaction between political will, strategy detailing, and worldwide collaboration shapes the direction of manageability endeavors. This investigation dives into the developing scene of political responsibilities to supportability, looking at key systems, difficulties, and open doors inborn chasing an additional reasonable and evenhanded future.

Global Structures and Arrangements:

The obligation to supportability on a worldwide scale is exemplified through different global structures and arrangements that set up for aggregate activity among countries.

Joined Countries Reasonable Improvement Objectives (SDGs): The SDGs, took on in 2015 by totally Joined Countries Part States, address a thorough and interconnected plan for worldwide turn of events. Involving 17 objectives and 169 focuses on, the SDGs envelop financial, social, and natural aspects. States overall have focused on accomplishing these objectives by 2030, cultivating a common vision for an additional economical and comprehensive world.

Paris Settlement on Environmental Change: The Paris Arrangement, embraced in 2015 under the Unified Countries Structure Show on Environmental Change (UNFCCC), is a milestone accord pointed toward restricting worldwide temperature climb to well under 2 degrees Celsius above pre-modern levels. Nations that are gatherings to the arrangement have focused on broadly resolved commitments (NDCs) illustrating their endeavors to diminish ozone harming substance outflows and upgrade strength to environment influences.

Show on Organic Variety (CBD): The CBD, laid out in 1992, addresses the preservation of biodiversity and the feasible utilization of its parts. Countries that are gatherings to the show focus on executing techniques to save natural variety, economically utilize its parts, and guarantee the fair and evenhanded sharing of advantages emerging from hereditary assets.

Sendai Structure for Catastrophe Hazard Decrease: Embraced in 2015, the Sendai System frames a 15-year methodology to diminish the dangers and effects of fiascos. It underscores the significance of incorporating debacle risk decrease into practical improvement endeavors and advancing strength at public and local area levels.

Public Responsibilities and Strategy Plan:
Political responsibilities to supportability manifest at the public level through the detailing of arrangements, techniques, and activity designs that line up with worldwide structures.

Public Supportable Improvement Systems: Numerous nations have created Public Economical Advancement Methodologies as a way to operationalize the SDGs at the public level. These systems articulate the country-explicit pathways to accomplishing reasonable turn of events, taking into account social, monetary, and ecological aspects.

Environment Activity Plans: because of the Paris Understanding, nations form environment activity plans framing their responsibilities to diminish ozone harming substance outflows, progress to sustainable power, and improve environment flexibility. These plans act as outlines for public endeavors to battle environmental change.

Biodiversity Preservation Plans: Legislatures foster biodiversity protection intends to address the targets of the CBD. These plans normally frame measures to secure and reestablish environments, save jeopardized species, and advance manageable practices that defend biodiversity.

Green Development and Round Economy Arrangements: A few countries embrace the idea of green development, coordinating ecological contemplations into financial improvement procedures. Roundabout economy strategies, which focus on the productive utilization of assets and the decrease of waste, line up with supportability objectives by elevating a regenerative way to deal with monetary exercises.

Provokes in Political Responsibilities to Supportability:
While political responsibilities to supportability address urgent forward moving steps, a few difficulties obstruct the viable execution of these responsibilities.

Absence of Political Will: The interpretation of political responsibilities into substantial activities frequently relies on the strength of political will. Now and again, state run administrations might focus on transient financial interests over long haul maintainability objectives, prompting delays or deficient execution of supportability measures.

Conflicting Arrangement Execution: The successful execution of supportability approaches requires consistency across government activities. Conflicting arrangements, clashing needs, and changes in authority can upset the coherence of supportability endeavors, thwarting advancement.

Personal stakes and Campaigning: Strong personal stakes, like those in the petroleum derivative industry or different areas with natural effects, can impact political choices and obstruct the reception of additional economical practices. Campaigning endeavors might oppose administrative changes that challenge laid out plans of action.

Asset Limitations: Carrying out maintainability gauges frequently requires critical monetary assets and mechanical speculations. Nations with restricted assets might confront difficulties in completely understanding their supportability responsibilities, prompting a possible uniqueness in the speed of progress among countries.

Worldwide Imbalances and Power Elements: The elements of worldwide administration now and again propagate disparities, with additional strong countries applying more noteworthy impact. This can prompt differences in the obligation to and execution of manageability measures, possibly fueling ecological difficulties.

Valuable open doors for Improved Political Responsibilities:

In the midst of difficulties, there are amazing chances to fortify political responsibilities to maintainability, encouraging more aggressive and powerful activities.

Public Mindfulness and Promotion: Uplifted public mindfulness and support assume a critical part in impacting political will. At the point when residents request supportability and consider pioneers responsible, legislatures are bound to focus on and execute strategies that line up with ecological and social objectives.

Global Coordinated effort: Fortifying worldwide cooperation can improve political responsibilities to supportability. Shared difficulties, for example, environmental change and biodiversity misfortune, require helpful endeavors. Cooperative drives, joint examination, and information sharing can intensify the effect of manageability measures.

Comprehensive Dynamic Cycles: Guaranteeing inclusivity in dynamic cycles adds to the authenticity and adequacy of supportability approaches. Comprehensive administration, including different partners, common society, and underestimated networks, encourages a more extensive viewpoint and advances fair arrangements.

Developments in Money and Innovation: Advancements in money and innovation offer chances to conquer asset requirements. Maintainable money components, like green securities and effect ventures, can prepare assets for maintainability projects. In the mean time, progressions in innovation give devices to additional proficient and economical practices.

Strategy Reconciliation Across Areas: Coordinating manageability contemplations across areas guarantees a thorough and intelligent way to deal with strategy definition. Perceiving the interconnectedness of social, monetary, and natural angles empowers legislatures to all the while foster comprehensive methodologies that address various components of maintainability.

Common Society and Non-Administrative Associations (NGOs):

Common society and non-legislative associations (NGOs) assume a crucial part in considering states responsible, upholding for maintainability, and driving positive change.

Observing and Responsibility: Common society associations frequently screen government activities, survey strategy execution, and consider legislatures responsible for their maintainability responsibilities. Straightforwardness and responsibility components fortify the viability of political vows.

Support for Strategy Change: NGOs participate in backing endeavors to impact strategy change, raise public mindfulness, and shape the political talk on maintainability. By giving proof based suggestions and preparing public help, these associations add to a more favorable strategy climate.

Local area Drove Drives: Grassroots developments and local area drove drives feature the potential for restricted supportability endeavors. These drives exhibit the substantial advantages of manageability rehearses at the local area level, impacting more extensive political stories and encouraging base up change.

6.3 International Cooperation on Climate Change

Global participation on environmental change has arisen as a basic despite heightening natural dangers. The complicated and interconnected nature of environmental change rises above public lines, requiring cooperative endeavors among countries to moderate its effects and adjust to the developing real factors of a warming planet. This investigation dives into the elements of worldwide collaboration on environmental change, analyzing key arrangements, challenges, and the advancing scene of worldwide endeavors to address this existential test.

Authentic Setting and Achievements:

The acknowledgment of environmental change as a worldwide concern picked up speed throughout the long term, prompting huge achievements in global collaboration.

Joined Countries Structure Show on Environmental Change (UNFCCC): Embraced in 1992, the UNFCCC laid out the central system for tending to environmental change at the worldwide level. The show's definitive goal is to settle ozone harming substance fixations in the environment at levels that forestall risky human obstruction with the environment framework.

Kyoto Convention: The Kyoto Convention, embraced in 1997 as an expansion of the UNFCCC, denoted an essential step in the right direction by setting restricting outflow decrease focuses for created nations. It presented the idea of legitimately restricting responsibilities to diminish ozone depleting substance discharges during the primary responsibility time frame (2008-2012).

Paris Understanding: The Paris Understanding, embraced in 2015, addresses a milestone accord inside the UNFCCC structure. Not at all like the Kyoto Convention, the Paris Understanding embraces a granular perspective, with each taking an interest country deciding its own broadly resolved commitments (NDCs) to relieve environmental change. The arrangement plans to restrict an Earth-wide temperature boost to well under 2 degrees Celsius above pre-modern levels, with endeavors to restrict the increment to 1.5 degrees Celsius.

Key Parts of Worldwide Participation:

Worldwide collaboration on environmental change includes a huge number of parts that by and large add to the worldwide reaction to this dire test.

Broadly Resolved Commitments (NDCs): NDCs are key to the Paris Arrangement, addressing the responsibilities made by every country to decrease its ozone harming substance discharges and improve strength to environment influences. Customary updates and improvements of NDCs are urged to reflect expanding desires after some time.

Environment Money: Monetary help is urgent for both moderation and variation endeavors, especially in non-industrial nations that face critical difficulties in tending to environmental change. The activation of environment finance includes commitments from created nations to help environment related undertakings and drives in agricultural countries.

Innovation Move and Limit Building: Working with the exchange of feasible advancements and building the limit of countries to embrace and carry out these advancements are indispensable parts of global participation. This move means to improve the versatility of weak countries and advance practical turn of events.

Transformation Methodologies: As environmental change influences manifest, variation techniques become progressively significant. Global participation upholds the turn of events and execution of versatile measures to safeguard networks, environments, and economies from the antagonistic impacts of environmental change.

Worldwide Stocktake: The Paris Understanding lays out a worldwide stocktake like clockwork to survey aggregate advancement toward its objectives. This cycle takes into account the recognizable proof of holes, regions for development, and the change of procedures to line up with the advancing comprehension of environmental change.

Challenges in Worldwide Collaboration:

In spite of progress, worldwide collaboration on environmental change faces impressive difficulties that ruin the full acknowledgment of worldwide environment objectives.

Different Public Interests: Countries fluctuate altogether in their financial needs, improvement stages, and asset gifts. Different public interests can prompt contentions in dealings, making it trying to arrive at agreement on aggressive and fair environment activity.

Verifiable Obligation: Discussions around authentic obligation regarding ozone harming substance discharges and environmental change frequently block collaboration. Non-industrial countries contend that created nations, generally liable for most of emanations, ought to bear a more noteworthy weight in tending to the effects and supporting relief and transformation endeavors in less evolved locales.

Environment Money Hole: While environment finance is a vital part of global collaboration, there stays a significant hole between the monetary responsibilities made by created nations and the genuine necessities of emerging countries. Overcoming this issue is fundamental for building trust and guaranteeing compelling worldwide activity.

Political Will and Authority Changes: The progression of environment responsibilities is helpless to changes in political administration and changes in public needs. An absence of supported political will and administration changes can bring about strategy inversions, influencing the direction of environment activity.

Lacking Execution and Authorization Components: The viability of peaceful accords depends on powerful systems for execution and implementation. Powerless implementation instruments, lacking observing, and the shortfall of punishments for rebelliousness can sabotage the adequacy of environment arrangements.

Potential open doors and Developing Elements:

In the midst of difficulties, there are potential open doors and developing elements that hold guarantee for upgraded worldwide collaboration on environmental change.

Recharged Responsibilities and Desire: The rising seriousness of environment related occasions has prodded reestablished responsibilities and increased aspiration from countries all over the planet. The acknowledgment of the dire requirement for definitive activity is driving nations to reevaluate and upgrade their environment responsibilities.

Development of Non-State Entertainers: Non-state entertainers, including urban communities, organizations, and common society associations, assume an undeniably powerful part in the worldwide environment exertion. Numerous urban communities and companies are setting aggressive discharges decrease targets and executing manageability drives, adding to base up tension for improved public and worldwide activity.

Mechanical Development and Joint effort: Fast progressions in clean energy advancements, like environmentally friendly power and energy stockpiling, present open doors for extraordinary change. Global joint effort in innovative work, as well as the sharing of mechanical arrangements, can speed up progress toward a low-carbon future.

Youth and Common Society Preparation: Youth-drove developments and common society assembly have intensified the earnestness of environment activity on a worldwide scale. These developments, exemplified by drives like Fridays for Future, stand out to the ethical basic of tending to environmental change for people in the future.

Multilateral Stages and Organizations: Multilateral stages and associations are working with joint effort on unambiguous parts of environment activity. Drives, for example, Mission Development, a worldwide work to speed up clean energy advancement, unite nations, organizations, and exploration establishments to address normal difficulties.

Worldwide Strength and Variation Endeavors:

As the effects of environmental change become progressively obvious, there is a developing accentuation on worldwide flexibility and variation endeavors.

Early Admonition Frameworks: Reinforcing early admonition frameworks for outrageous climate occasions, like storms, floods, and dry spells, is urgent for lessening the dangers and effects of environment related catastrophes. Global joint effort upholds the turn of events and execution of vigorous early advance notice systems.

Nature-Based Arrangements: Nature-based arrangements, including reforestation, feasible land the executives, and the assurance of biological systems, add to both moderation and variation endeavors. Global collaboration works with the sharing of information and best practices in executing nature-based arrangements.

Limit Working for Weak Countries: Weak countries, especially little island states and least created nations, require improved ability to adapt to the effects of environmental change. Global participation centers around building the versatile limit of these countries through monetary help, innovation move, and information sharing.

Chapter 7

Geopolitical Realignment

International realignment is an unpredictable cycle that includes shifts in worldwide power designs, partnerships, and key interests among countries. This peculiarity is dynamic, driven by developing international, financial, and innovative powers. The world has seen a few occasions of international realignment since forever ago, each formed by international, financial, and mechanical changes. This investigation dives into the contemporary scene of international realignment, analyzing key elements, arising patterns, and their suggestions on the worldwide stage.

Changing Elements of Worldwide Power:

One of the focal components of international realignment is the changing elements of worldwide power. Customary power structures, frequently described by a bipolar or unipolar dissemination, have seen shifts as of late. The ascent of new monetary forces to be reckoned with, changes in military abilities, and the rise of local entertainers add to the mind boggling snare of worldwide power elements.

Ascent of China: China's rising as a worldwide monetary force to be reckoned with has been a characterizing component of contemporary international realignment. With quick industrialization, innovative headways, and key speculations, China has changed from a territorial player to a significant worldwide entertainer. This shift difficulties the conventional strength of Western powers and acquaints a multipolar aspect with worldwide international relations.

Resurgence of Russia: Russia's resurgence as an international player has changed the overall influence in Eurasia and then some. Self-assured activities in territorial contentions, key organizations, and discretionary moves have situated Russia as a huge power testing the unipolar world request that arose after the Virus War.

Multipolarity and Territorial Powers: Past China and Russia, other local powers are likewise stating their impact. India's monetary development, Brazil's part in South America, and the rising conspicuousness of nations like Turkey and Iran add to the multipolar circulation of force. Local entertainers assume significant parts in molding international realignment, affecting both territorial and worldwide elements.

Financial Interdependencies and Unions:

International realignment is unpredictably connected with financial interdependencies and the development of collusions. Financial variables assume a critical part in molding the international scene, cultivating collaboration or contest among countries.

Belt and Street Drive (BRI): China's aggressive Belt and Street Drive is a perfect representation of how financial interests drive international realignment. Through foundation projects, economic accords, and speculations, China tries to universally extend its monetary impact. The BRI cultivates new collusions and associations, reshaping international elements across Asia, Africa, and Europe.

Monetary Coalitions and Collusions: Local financial coalitions and partnerships, like the European Association, ASEAN, and the African Association, add to international realignment by making helpful structures. These alliances upgrade monetary mix, cultivate political ties, and impact international results. The strength of monetary partnerships frequently converts into political influence on the worldwide stage.

Mechanical Movements and Network protection Concerns:

The continuous mechanical transformation acquaints new aspects with international realignment, especially in the domains of network protection, man-made brainpower, and advanced framework.

Network protection and Data Fighting: The significance of online protection has flooded as countries perceive the essential meaning of data fighting. Digital capacities and the capacity to impact accounts in the advanced domain have become basic parts of international power. States take part in digital activities to shield public interests, gain knowledge, and apply impact over enemies.

Mechanical Advancement and Key Ventures: Countries competing for international impact progressively center around mechanical development and the improvement of vital enterprises. Spaces like 5G innovation, man-made consciousness, and quantum processing are becoming landmarks for worldwide incomparability. Command over these innovations can shape monetary seriousness and military abilities.

Moving Unions and Worldwide Administration Difficulties:

The liquid idea of international realignment is reflected in the moving unions and the difficulties looked by worldwide administration structures. Customary unions are being rethought, and new associations are arising in light of shared interests and key objectives.

Disparity in Partnerships: Customary collusions, like NATO, are encountering inside strains as part states rethink their international needs. Difference in essential interests, clashing perspectives on security dangers, and financial contemplations add to the reconsideration of well established collusions. Countries look for adaptable associations that line up with their developing international goals.

Worldwide Administration Holes: The changing international scene presents difficulties to existing worldwide administration structures. Global associations, including the Unified Countries, face troubles in resolving complex issues, for example, environmental change, pandemics, and digital dangers. The shortfall of agreement among significant powers frustrates successful worldwide administration, leaving basic difficulties neglected.

Local Struggles and Intermediary Wars:
International realignment frequently appears in local contentions and intermediary wars, where significant powers support contradicting groups to propel their essential advantages. These contentions become fields for international rivalry, with sweeping ramifications for the impacted districts and worldwide soundness.

Center East Elements: The Center East represents the effect of international realignment on local struggles. The association of significant powers in clashes in Syria, Yemen, and different areas of interest mirrors their international advantages in the locale. Rivalry for impact, admittance to assets, and key situating add to the complicated elements molding the Center East.

Ukraine and Eastern Europe: The contention in Ukraine and strains in Eastern Europe feature international competitions, especially among Russia and Western powers. The essential meaning of the locale, energy contemplations, and verifiable variables add to the complex international realignment unfurling in Eastern Europe.

Suggestions for Worldwide Security and Steadiness:
The international realignment in progress has significant ramifications for worldwide security and steadiness. The potential for clashes, the redefinition of safety dangers, and the difficulties presented by modern security issues make a perplexing and dubious worldwide security scene.

Military Modernization and Key Acting: Countries took part in international realignment frequently focus on military modernization and vital posing. The improvement of cutting edge military capacities, atomic munititions stockpiles, and the foundation of army installations in essential locales add to a more serious and possibly unpredictable worldwide security climate.

Contemporary Security Dangers: International realignment presents forward thinking security dangers, including online protection dangers, pandemics, and environmental change. These dangers rise above public boundaries and require agreeable worldwide reactions. The viability of worldwide administration in tending to these difficulties is essential for keeping up with security and solidness.

Compassionate Outcomes: Provincial contentions coming about because of international realignment have critical philanthropic results. Dislodging, displaced person emergencies, and the disintegration of basic freedoms are much of the time side-effects of international rivalry. The global local area's capacity to address philanthropic difficulties is dependent upon viable collaboration and political arrangements.

7.1 Changes in Alliances and Power Dynamics

Changes in coalitions and power elements are signs of the developing international scene, where the multifaceted dance of countries and moving loyalties reclassifies worldwide connections. The global request observers ceaseless change as nations reconsider their essential advantages, fashion new organizations, and explore international difficulties. This investigation dives into the contemporary changes in partnerships and power elements, analyzing the driving variables, key movements, and the ramifications for worldwide strength.

Rise of Key Organizations:

One outstanding pattern in the domain of collusions is the development of key associations that rise above conventional international limits. Countries are progressively looking for unions in view of shared interests, financial open doors, and common security concerns as opposed to unbending philosophical affiliations.

Financial Interests as an Impetus: Monetary contemplations assume a critical part in forming key organizations. Nations with correlative economies, innovative qualities, or asset conditions frequently structure partnerships to use each other's assets. Monetary organizations make interdependencies that can encourage dependability and participation among countries.

Provincial Collusions: Territorial partnerships have acquired conspicuousness as countries perceive the competitive edges of working together with neighbors. Territorial groupings, like the Relationship of Southeast Asian Countries (ASEAN), the African Association, and the Middle Easterner Association, act as stages for collaboration on monetary, security, and formative issues. These coalitions add to provincial solidness and impact worldwide undertakings.

Forward thinking Unions: Past conventional state-to-state partnerships, contemporary coalitions are forming the international scene. Coalitions with non-state entertainers, including global companies, persuasive people, and non-administrative associations (NGOs), impact dynamic cycles and add to the redefinition of force elements.

Changes in Worldwide Power Habitats:

The dispersion of worldwide power is going through critical movements, testing laid out standards and making ready for new focuses of impact. Customary powers are confronting contest from rising countries, modifying the elements of worldwide relations.

Ascent of China: China's command as a worldwide power addresses perhaps of the most significant change in ongoing many years. The country's financial ability, mechanical headways, and emphatic discretion have situated it as a central part in foreign relations. China's Belt and Street Drive (BRI) has extended its impact by encouraging monetary binds with various countries, reshaping the customary power structure overwhelmed by the West.

Multipolarity: The world is progressing toward a more multipolar conveyance of force, with a few countries applying huge impact. Close by the US and China, local powers like India, Russia, Brazil, and Turkey are assuming vital parts in molding worldwide issues. This multipolarity brings intricacy and ease into global relations.

Difficulties to Unipolarity: The unipolar world request that arose after the Virus Battle, with the US as the prevalent superpower, is confronting difficulties. The disintegration of unipolarity is apparent in the moving partnerships and the decisiveness of other significant powers. The worldwide framework is adjusting to oblige a more expanded power structure.

International Realignment and Territorial Areas of interest:

International realignment frequently appears in territorial areas of interest where vital interests unite and contending powers look for impact. Provincial contentions become fields for international rivalry, compounding strains and molding the more extensive power elements.

Center East Elements: The Center East remaining parts a point of convergence of international realignment, described by complex unions and clashes. The contribution of worldwide and provincial powers in clashes like those in Syria, Yemen, and Iraq reflects vital moving and the quest for international interests. The district's importance, driven by energy assets and vital areas, draws in the consideration of key part.

Eastern Europe and Russia's Effective reach: Eastern Europe, especially Ukraine, is a locale where international realignment is articulated. Russia's self-assured activities in the district, including the extension of Crimea, have prompted pressures with Western abilities. Eastern European nations explore the sensitive harmony between noteworthy binds with Russia and goals for closer arrangement with Western organizations.

Security Coalitions and Safeguard Collaboration:

Security coalitions and safeguard collaboration plans keep on advancing as countries adjust to arising dangers and international difficulties. The idea of safety coalitions mirrors the changing person of contentions and the requirement for cooperative reactions.

NATO's Transformation: The North Atlantic Deal Association (NATO), a foundation of Cold Conflict time security unions, has adjusted to contemporary difficulties. The coalition tends to a scope of dangers, including digital dangers and cross breed fighting, mirroring a more extensive comprehension of safety concerns. NATO's associations with non-part states and agreeable endeavors in regions like counterterrorism show its advancing job.

Moving Security Partnerships in Asia: Asia is seeing eminent changes in security unions, driven by provincial power elements and regional debates. The Quad, containing the US, Japan, India, and Australia, has acquired noticeable quality as a security discussion pointed toward encouraging strength in the Indo-Pacific. The essential significance of the area has prompted different security organizations and arrangements.

Suggestions for Worldwide Steadiness and Discretion:

Changes in coalitions and power elements have broad ramifications for worldwide dependability and discretionary relations. The ease of the international scene presents vulnerabilities and difficulties that require nuanced discretionary methodologies.

Strategic Difficult exercises: Countries take part in fragile difficult exercises as they explore moving coalitions. Tact turns into an intricate dance of seeking after essential interests, keeping up with adaptability, and adjusting to changing international conditions. Capable strategy is fundamental to oversee assorted connections and stay away from ensnarements in clashes.

Worldwide Administration Difficulties: The advancing power elements present difficulties to worldwide administration structures. Worldwide associations and establishments face challenges in resolving issues that require aggregate activity, for example, environmental change, pandemics, and movement. The adequacy of worldwide administration is dependent upon the capacity of countries to team up in spite of disparate interests.

Potential for Struggle and Collaboration: While changes in unions can add to territorial dependability, they likewise convey the gamble of contention. Contending interests, regional questions, and authentic enmities might raise pressures. Simultaneously, essential participation and discretionary exchange offer roads for compromise and cooperative critical thinking.

7.2 Emerging Global Leaders

The worldwide scene is seeing the rise of new pioneers who are reshaping the elements of global relations, adding to a more multipolar world request. These arising pioneers, both on the public and global stage, are described by their monetary ability, innovative progressions, strategic insight, and the capacity to explore complex international difficulties. This investigation digs into the profiles of a portion of the vital arising worldwide pioneers and dissects their effect on the developing global scene.

1. **China's Ascent under Xi Jinping:**
   China, under the initiative of President Xi Jinping, has arisen as a transcendent worldwide player, testing laid out standards and stating its impact across various spaces. Xi's authority has been set apart by aggressive drives, including the Belt and Street Drive (BRI), which plans to improve China's financial network with the world. The country's financial ability, mechanical headways, and confident international strategy have situated China as a vital participant in foreign relations. As China explores complex associations with significant powers, especially the US, its impact keeps on developing, molding the forms of the worldwide request.

2. **India's Job under Narendra Modi:**
   State head Narendra Modi has pushed India into the worldwide spotlight, controlling the country towards monetary development, vital associations, and mechanical progressions. Modi's administration has underscored monetary changes, framework advancement, and strategic effort. India's consideration in discussions like the Quad, close by the US, Japan, and Australia, highlights its rising impact in the Indo-Pacific district. The country's essential significance, joined with an energetic segment and a blossoming tech industry, positions India as a central member in forming the international scene before long.

3. **Brazil's Strategic Effort with Jair Bolsonaro:**
   President Jair Bolsonaro has brought a change in outlook to Brazil's international

strategy, underscoring nearer attaches with worldwide powers and encouraging monetary organizations. Brazil's decisive position in worldwide gatherings, especially on ecological issues and exchange, mirrors Bolsonaro's obligation to public interests. The country's immense normal assets, rural strength, and territorial impact add to its rise as a critical player in the worldwide field. Brazil's discretionary drives expect to reinforce its situation in key global conversations, going from environmental change to monetary collaboration.

4. **Russia's Confidence with Vladimir Putin:**
President Vladimir Putin keeps on molding Russia's job on the worldwide stage, underscoring military modernization, local impact, and vital associations. Russia's self-assured activities in Eastern Europe, the Center East, and Africa highlight its endeavors to recapture international noticeable quality. Putin's administration style, portrayed by a realistic way to deal with power governmental issues, has situated Russia as a central participant in molding worldwide security elements. Notwithstanding confronting difficulties and analysis, Putin's Russia stays a strong power in foreign relations, impacting conversations on security, energy, and local dependability.

5. **Turkey's Advancing Job under Recep Tayyip Erdoğan:**
President Recep Tayyip Erdoğan has changed Turkey's international strategy, stating its impact in the Center East, North Africa, and then some. Erdoğan's initiative has been set apart by a more decisive and free position, testing conventional coalitions and chasing after Turkey's public advantages. The country's international area, military abilities, and verifiable ties add to its developing impact in provincial and worldwide undertakings. Turkey's part in clashes, for example, those in Syria and Libya mirrors its developing situation as a central member in molding the international scene.

6. **South Korea's Strategic Reach with Moon Jae-in:**
President Moon Jae-in has guided South Korea's conciliatory endeavors towards encouraging harmony and security in the Korean Landmass, while additionally extending its worldwide impact. Moon's accentuation on between Korean exchange and commitment has earned worldwide consideration, adding to a defrost in relations among North and South Korea. South Korea's financial strength, mechanical development, and obligation to tending to worldwide difficulties, for example, environmental change and general wellbeing, position it as a rising political power in East Asia and then some.

7. **Saudi Arabia's Change Plan under Mohammed receptacle Salman:**
Crown Ruler Mohammed receptacle Salman's initiative in Saudi Arabia has achieved a groundbreaking plan known as Vision 2030, pointed toward enhancing the nation's economy and diminishing its reliance on oil.
The Crown Sovereign's decisive methodology in provincial contentions and political drives has situated Saudi Arabia as a central participant in the Center

East. The country's financial changes, social changes, and vital associations add to its developing job in forming the international scene of the district.

8. **Nigeria's Impact in Africa with Muhammadu Buhari:**

President Muhammadu Buhari plays had a huge impact in forming Nigeria's impact inside the African mainland. As the most crowded country in Africa, Nigeria's monetary strength, provincial administration, and obligation to addressing security challenges add to its significant job. Buhari's initiative has centered around issues like counterterrorism, monetary turn of events, and discretionary commitment inside Africa and on the worldwide stage, situating Nigeria as a central participant in molding the fate of the mainland.

7.3 The Role of International Organizations

Worldwide associations assume a crucial part in forming the elements of worldwide administration, cultivating collaboration among countries, and tending to shared difficulties that rise above borders. In an undeniably interconnected world, these associations act as discussions for discretionary exchange, stages for aggregate activity, and components for organizing reactions to complex issues. This investigation digs into the multi-layered job of worldwide associations, looking at their capabilities, challenges, and the developing scene of worldwide administration.

Elements of Global Associations:

Worldwide associations serve different capabilities that add to the upkeep of harmony, advancement of financial turn of events, security of common liberties, and tending to worldwide difficulties. These capabilities can be comprehensively ordered into discretionary, financial, social, and compassionate jobs.

Strategic Capabilities: Worldwide associations give stages to discretionary discourse and compromise. Elements like the Assembled Countries (UN) work with discussions among part states, attempting to forestall clashes, resolve debates, and advance global harmony and security. Conciliatory capabilities likewise incorporate the foundation of settlements, shows, and arrangements that shape the direct of countries in different circles.

Financial Capabilities: Associations like the Global Money related Asset (IMF) and the World Bank add to worldwide monetary dependability and improvement. They give monetary help, strategy guidance, and specialized skill to part nations, cultivating financial development and tending to difficulties like destitution, imbalance, and monetary emergencies. Financial capabilities additionally include planning endeavors to advance deregulation, venture, and reasonable turn of events.

Social Capabilities: Global associations assume an essential part in advancing social government assistance and common liberties. Elements like the World Wellbeing Association (WHO) work to address worldwide wellbeing challenges, coordinate reactions to pandemics, and upgrade medical care frameworks around the world. Moreover, associations like the Unified Countries Instructive, Logical and Social

Association (UNESCO) center around cultivating training, social trade, and logical collaboration.

Philanthropic Capabilities: in the midst of emergencies, worldwide associations assume a fundamental part in giving helpful help. Organizations like the Assembled Countries High Magistrate for Evacuees (UNHCR) and the Worldwide Board of trustees of the Red Cross (ICRC) work to mitigate the enduring of exiles, uprooted people, and those impacted by clashes or catastrophic events. Helpful capabilities include conveying help, safeguarding weak populaces, and advancing human pride.

Challenges Confronting Worldwide Associations:

Regardless of their vital jobs, worldwide associations face a scope of difficulties that influence their viability and capacity to resolve worldwide issues. These difficulties include:

Political Fracture: Global associations frequently wrestle with political discontinuity, where part states might have dissimilar interests and needs. The Assembled Countries Security Chamber (UNSC), for example, can confront gridlock while blackball using individuals seek after clashing plans, impeding convenient and unequivocal activity on major problems.

Restricted Authorization Components: Numerous peaceful accords and shows depend on deliberate consistence, lacking hearty implementation systems. This postures difficulties in guaranteeing that part states stick to their responsibilities, particularly in regions like ecological security, basic freedoms, and arms control.

Asset Imperatives: Worldwide associations habitually face asset requirements that influence their capacity to thoroughly address worldwide difficulties. Subsidizing deficiencies can ruin helpful endeavors, limit improvement drives, and obstruct reactions to emergencies. Reliance on deliberate commitments might make variations in monetary help among part states.

Disintegration of Multilateralism: The ascent of unilateralism and patriot feelings in certain nations has prompted a difficult climate for multilateral collaboration. A few countries focus on their singular advantages over aggregate activity, subverting the standards of multilateralism and debilitating the viability of worldwide associations.

The Advancing Scene of Worldwide Administration:

The scene of worldwide administration is developing, reflecting changing power elements, mechanical progressions, and the rise of new entertainers. A few patterns shape the eventual fate of worldwide associations:

Consideration of Non-State Entertainers: The job of non-state entertainers, including worldwide partnerships, common society associations, and charitable establishments, is progressively perceived in worldwide administration. These elements contribute aptitude, assets, and support to address complex difficulties, enhancing the endeavors of customary state-driven global associations.

Mechanical Developments: Innovative headways, including advanced correspondence, man-made brainpower, and information investigation, are impacting the manner in which worldwide associations work. These advancements upgrade coordination, work with data trade, and deal new instruments for resolving worldwide issues, for example, online protection, environmental change checking, and general wellbeing.

Center around Practical Turn of events: There is a developing accentuation on reasonable improvement as a core value for worldwide administration. Worldwide associations are adjusting their endeavors to the Unified Countries Feasible Improvement Objectives (SDGs), which address key difficulties, for example, neediness, disparity, environmental change, and natural debasement.

Local Collaboration: Territorial associations and partnerships assume an undeniably huge part in worldwide administration. Provincial bodies, like the European Association (EU), ASEAN, and the African Association, work to address shared difficulties inside their separate geological regions and add to the general dependability and thriving of the global framework.

Chapter 8

Challenges and Opportunities

Exploring the perplexing scene of the contemporary world, countries wrestle with a heap of difficulties and open doors that shape their directions. These difficulties are multi-layered, traversing international, financial, innovative, and cultural aspects. However, inside the complexities of these difficulties lie valuable open doors for development, joint effort, and groundbreaking change. This investigation digs into the interconnected difficulties and valuable open doors that characterize the worldwide scene, delineating how countries can adjust and flourish in the midst of vulnerability.

1. **International Difficulties:**
   In the domain of international affairs, countries face a large group of difficulties that test political versatility and key discernment. Rising pressures between significant powers, regional debates, and the disintegration of longstanding coalitions add to a climate of international vulnerability. The test lies in overseeing prompt contentions as well as in laying out systems for supported collaboration and forestalling the heightening of questions into worldwide emergencies.
   A chance for Strategic Development: In the midst of international difficulties, there exists a chance for countries to take part in conciliatory development. Building multilateral systems, improving compromise components, and encouraging discourse can prepare for additional steady and agreeable worldwide relations. Shrewd and spry tact is fundamental to explore the complex snare of international elements and look for shared belief.

2. **Financial Elements and Disparities:**
   Financial difficulties, set apart by differences in riches, exchange lopsided characteristics, and the effect of worldwide monetary slumps, present significant obstacles for countries taking a stab at supported development and improvement. Tending to monetary imbalances inside and among nations isn't just an ethical objective yet additionally critical for cultivating worldwide security.
   A chance for Comprehensive Development: The monetary difficulties of

today present a chance for countries to focus on comprehensive development. Carrying out strategies that address pay imbalance, elevate admittance to instruction and medical services, and support manageable monetary practices can make a more impartial and strong worldwide economy. Cooperative endeavors through worldwide associations can enhance the effect of such drives.

3. **Mechanical Disturbances and Security Concerns:**
Quick mechanical headways bring the two potential open doors and difficulties, as countries wrestle with the groundbreaking force of man-made consciousness, network safety dangers, and the moral ramifications of arising innovations. Offsetting development with security and moral contemplations turns into a fragile errand, requiring proactive measures to outfit the advantages of innovation while relieving likely dangers.

A chance for Moral Tech Administration: Countries have the valuable chance to situate themselves as pioneers in moral innovation administration. Laying out strong administrative structures, cultivating worldwide collaboration on network protection, and resolving issues of protection and information administration can make a safe and mindful innovative scene. By forming the story around mechanical progressions, countries can drive development that lines up with cultural qualities.

4. **Ecological Supportability and Environmental Change:**
The worldwide ecological emergency, driven by environmental change, deforestation, and contamination, represents an existential danger that rises above public lines. Rising ocean levels, outrageous climate occasions, and the exhaustion of normal assets request pressing and composed activity to moderate the effect of environmental change and safeguard the planet for people in the future.

A chance for Green Development: The basic of ecological supportability presents a chance for countries to lead in green advancement. Putting resources into sustainable power, carrying out maintainable farming practices, and cultivating eco-accommodating advancements might address natural difficulties at any point as well as invigorate monetary development. Global joint effort through drives like the Paris Arrangement highlights the aggregate liability to shield the planet.

5. **Social and Segment Movements:**
Segment changes, including maturing populaces and movement designs, present difficulties to social designs and medical care frameworks. Cultural movements, driven by social changes and developing qualities, require variation to guarantee social union and inclusivity.

A chance for Comprehensive Social Strategies: Countries can jump all over the chance to carry out comprehensive social strategies that address the requirements of different populaces. Embracing variety, advancing orientation correspondence, and putting resources into social projects that help weak networks add to social solidness. By perceiving and celebrating social variety, countries can fabricate tough social orders that flourish with inclusivity.

6. **General Wellbeing and Worldwide Pandemics:**

The new worldwide pandemic has highlighted the interconnected idea of general wellbeing challenges. Containing the spread of irresistible sicknesses, guaranteeing admittance to medical care, and tending to the emotional well-being effect of emergencies require composed worldwide endeavors.

A chance for Worldwide Wellbeing Joint effort: The difficulties presented by general wellbeing emergencies offer a chance for countries to reinforce worldwide wellbeing cooperation. Putting resources into medical services foundation, sharing clinical information and assets, and supporting global associations like the World Wellbeing Association (WHO) can upgrade the aggregate capacity to answer wellbeing crises. Cooperative examination, immunization circulation, and pandemic readiness are vital parts of worldwide wellbeing participation.

8.1 Unforeseen Challenges in the New Political Landscape

The beginning of another political scene frequently brings expectation and vulnerability as countries wrestle with unexpected difficulties that arise following political advances, changes in power elements, or worldwide occasions. These difficulties, unexpected and complex, test the strength of political frameworks, conciliatory relations, and cultural designs. This investigation dives into the unanticipated difficulties that can emerge in the new political scene, analyzing their diverse nature and the ramifications for countries exploring unfamiliar waters.

1. **Worldwide Wellbeing Emergencies:**
   The rise of a worldwide wellbeing emergency, as seen with the Coronavirus pandemic, addresses an imposing test that can reshape political scenes. The fast spread of irresistible infections challenges borders, presenting phenomenal dangers to general wellbeing, economies, and political strength. Such emergencies request quick and facilitated reactions, testing the readiness and flexibility of states.

   Influence on Administration: The unanticipated test of a worldwide wellbeing emergency puts huge strain on administration structures. Legislatures should offset general wellbeing measures with financial soundness, explore vulnerabilities in medical services frameworks, and settle on basic choices despite advancing conditions. Viable emergency the executives turns into a litmus test for political initiative.

   Political Strain: Worldwide wellbeing emergencies can strain conciliatory relations as countries wrestle with the intricacies of global participation, data sharing, and asset portion. The requirement for fortitude even with a common danger can either reinforce or strain discretionary ties, contingent upon the capacity of countries to really team up.

2. **Monetary Shocks and Disturbances:**
Unexpected monetary shocks, whether set off by worldwide downturns, monetary emergencies, or outside shocks, present critical difficulties for policymakers. The financial aftermath from unanticipated occasions can disturb jobs, strain social wellbeing nets, and challenge the strength of political frameworks.

Social Agitation and Imbalance: Monetary shocks frequently intensify existing disparities and add to social distress. Disturbances in work, pay imbalance, and abberations in admittance to assets can fuel discontent among populaces. Political pioneers should wrestle with the fragile assignment of tending to financial difficulties while keeping up with social attachment.

Strategy Reactions: Unexpected monetary difficulties require dexterous arrangement reactions. States should adjust financial and money related approaches, execute improvement gauges, and establish changes to relieve the effect on organizations and people. The viability of strategy reactions assumes an essential part in forming public view of political authority.

3. **Mechanical Interruptions and Online protection Dangers:**
The fast speed of mechanical progressions brings unexpected difficulties, especially in the domain of network protection. Digital dangers, going from state-supported assaults to cybercrime, can upset basic framework, compromise public safety, and challenge the actual texture of administration.

Public safety Concerns: Online protection dangers present huge public safety worries, as vindictive entertainers target touchy government organizations, basic foundation, and safeguard frameworks. The unexpected test lies in creating vigorous network protection measures to shield against advancing and complex digital dangers.

Protection and Advanced Freedoms: The innovative scene acquaints difficulties related with security and computerized privileges. State run administrations should explore the sensitive harmony between guaranteeing public safety and protecting residents' security. Unexpected advancements in innovation might require the creation or variation of legitimate structures to address arising concerns.

4. **Social and Social Movements:**
Unanticipated social and social movements, driven by segment changes, generational perspectives, or surprising occasions, can reshape the political scene. Developments for civil rights, social changes, or changes in general assessment can introduce difficulties and amazing open doors for political pioneers.

Generational Elements: Changing perspectives and values across ages can impact political talk and policymaking. Unexpected changes in generational elements might require political pioneers to adjust their correspondence systems, strategy needs, and commitment techniques to resound with developing cultural standards.

Social Developments: The rise of grassroots social developments, frequently ignited by unexpected occasions or cultural complaints, can shape political plans and request foundational change. Exploring the effect of social developments requires political pioneers to draw in with assorted viewpoints, address complaints, and figure out something worth agreeing on to forestall polarization.

5. **Natural Emergencies and Environmental Change:**

The rising recurrence and power of ecological emergencies, including catastrophic events and the effects of environmental change, present unexpected difficulties that rise above borders. Political pioneers should wrestle with the prompt outcomes of ecological emergencies and foster long haul systems for maintainability.

Asset The board: Natural emergencies, for example, outrageous climate occasions or asset shortage, present difficulties to asset the executives and portion. The unexpected idea of these emergencies requires versatile techniques to guarantee the flexibility of networks and economies.

Worldwide Collaboration: Tending to natural difficulties requires global participation. Political pioneers should explore the intricacies of worldwide environment arrangements, arrange responsibilities, and team up on drives to alleviate the effect of environmental change. The unanticipated test lies in cultivating aggregate activity in the midst of assorted public interests.

6. **Pandemic Readiness and Worldwide Wellbeing Administration:**

While pandemics fall under the more extensive class of worldwide wellbeing emergencies, the particular test of pandemic readiness and worldwide wellbeing administration warrants unmistakable thought. The eccentricism of irresistible illnesses requires consistent transformation of medical care frameworks, worldwide coordinated effort, and powerful administration structures.

Medical care Framework: Unexpected difficulties in pandemic readiness feature the requirement for vigorous medical services foundation. State run administrations should put resources into medical care frameworks, including observation, testing, and therapy capacities, to guarantee strength despite unexpected wellbeing dangers.

Worldwide Joint effort: Worldwide wellbeing administration requires viable global cooperation, data sharing, and facilitated reactions. The test lies in laying out systems for quick and straightforward correspondence, asset sharing, and cooperative examination to address arising wellbeing dangers.

8.2 Opportunities for Collaboration and Innovation

In the interconnected and quickly developing scene of the 21st hundred years, countries are given remarkable open doors for joint effort and advancement. These open doors, established in shared difficulties and progressions in innovation, give the establishment to producing new ways toward feasible turn of events, financial development, and worldwide dependability. This investigation digs into the diverse open doors that emerge when countries team up and enhance, analyzing how aggregate endeavors can drive positive change on the worldwide stage.

1. **Logical and Mechanical Joint effort:**
   One of the main open doors for countries lies in the domain of logical and mechanical joint effort. In a time set apart by fast headways in fields like man-made brainpower, biotechnology, and environmentally friendly power, countries can enhance their advancement by pooling assets, skill, and examination endeavors. Cooperative drives in logical investigation, space investigation, and clinical exploration speed up progress as well as address worldwide difficulties that rise above public boundaries.

   Worldwide Exploration Associations: Cooperative examination drives, worked with by global associations and joint endeavors, permit countries to use each other's assets. Shared information, assets, and mastery add to forward leaps in medication, ecological science, and innovation, cultivating a culture of open development.

   Space Investigation and Advancement: The cooperative investigation of room epitomizes the potential for global collaboration. Projects like the Global Space Station (ISS) include commitments from various countries, exhibiting how shared objectives in space investigation lead to mechanical developments, logical revelations, and a mutual perspective of the universe.

2. **Exchange and Monetary Organizations:**
   Monetary coordinated effort and organizations offer countries the chance to tackle the advantages of globalization, drive financial development, and improve the thriving of their residents. Reciprocal and multilateral economic accords make a structure for the trading of merchandise, administrations, and ventures, encouraging financial reliance and dependability.

   International alliances: Partaking in international alliances empowers countries to get to bigger business sectors, increment the productivity of creation, and advance specialization. Cooperative financial structures, like the European Association (EU), give a model to how nations can pool assets and work with exchange to the shared advantage, everything being equal.

   Framework Improvement: Cooperative foundation projects, for example, cross-line transportation organizations and energy lattices, advance monetary reconciliation and provincial dependability. Countries can all in all put resources into projects that upgrade availability, work with exchange, and prod monetary advancement across borders.

3. **Environmental Change Relief and Reasonable Turn of events:**
   Tending to the worldwide test of environmental change requires cooperative endeavors to relieve ecological effect, advance manageability, and progress to low-carbon economies. Countries have the chance to spearhead inventive

arrangements, share best practices, and all in all work toward a more manageable future.

Environmentally friendly power Cooperation: Cooperative drives in sustainable power, for example, joint exploration projects and the sharing of innovation, drive the change to clean energy sources. Countries can cooperate to create and execute manageable energy arrangements, decreasing reliance on petroleum derivatives and alleviating the effect of environmental change.

Peaceful accords: Cooperation in peaceful accords, like the Paris Understanding, gives a system to countries to all in all address environmental change. Cooperative responsibilities to lessen ozone depleting substance discharges, safeguard biodiversity, and elevate supportable improvement add to a worldwide work to protect the climate.

4. **Emergency Reaction and Compassionate Cooperation:**

Worldwide difficulties, whether catastrophic events, pandemics, or compassionate emergencies, feature the requirement for countries to team up in emergency reaction and philanthropic endeavors. Shared assets, ability, and composed reactions are fundamental for tending to emergencies that rise above public limits.

Helpful Guide and Calamity Alleviation: Cooperative endeavors in philanthropic guide and catastrophe alleviation include countries cooperating to give help to impacted locales. Joint drives can incorporate the sharing of assets, aptitude, and calculated help to answer really to emergencies and mitigate human misery.

Pandemic Readiness: The new worldwide reaction to the Coronavirus pandemic highlights the significance of global cooperation in pandemic readiness. Countries can team up on immunization improvement, share clinical skill, and direction reactions to guarantee an aggregate and compelling way to deal with worldwide wellbeing emergencies.

5. **Social and Instructive Trades:**

Social and instructive trades give countries the chance to cultivate shared understanding, fortify individuals to-individuals associations, and advance a feeling of worldwide citizenship. Cooperative drives in training, expressions, and social trade add to building spans between countries.

Understudy Trade Projects: Cooperative understudy trade programs permit people to concentrate on in various nations, advancing culturally diverse comprehension and making an organization of worldwide residents. Openness to assorted points of view cultivates advancement and plans people to explore an interconnected world.

Social Tact: Cooperative social discretion drives, like global celebrations, creative coordinated efforts, and comprehensive developments, add to building spans between countries. Shared social encounters cultivate a feeling of normal humankind and work with discourse, even in the midst of political pressure.

6. **Security and Counterterrorism Participation:**

Guaranteeing worldwide security requires cooperative endeavors to address transnational dangers, like psychological warfare, cybercrime, and coordinated wrongdoing. Countries can pool knowledge assets, coordinate policing, and take part in joint military activities to improve aggregate security.

Knowledge Sharing: Cooperative insight sharing is urgent in tending to security dangers that rise above borders. Countries can cooperate to share data on arising dangers, forestall fear monger exercises, and counter digital dangers, adding to a more secure worldwide climate.

Military Coalitions: Security cooperation is exemplified by military unions like NATO, where part countries focus on aggregate safeguard. Joint military activities, vital coordination, and the sharing of military capacities improve the security stance of part states and add to discouragement.

8.3 Building a Resilient Global System

Despite developing difficulties and vulnerabilities, the basic to construct a strong worldwide framework has become more articulated than any other time in recent memory. A strong worldwide framework is one that can endure shocks, adjust to change, and encourage reasonable turn of events. This includes tending to prompt emergencies as well as sustaining the establishments for long haul soundness, participation, and advancement. This investigation dives into the vital components of building a strong worldwide framework, incorporating monetary, natural, social, and innovative aspects.

1. **Monetary Flexibility:**

   Monetary flexibility is basic to a stable worldwide framework. Countries should endeavor to make economies that can weather conditions shocks, endure slumps, and advance comprehensive development. This requires vital preparation, powerful monetary frameworks, and worldwide participation to guarantee the dependability of the worldwide economy.

   Broadening of Economies: Building monetary strength includes differentiating public economies to decrease reliance on unambiguous areas. Countries can put resources into a scope of ventures, from innovation to sustainable power, cultivating an additional versatile and strong financial base.

   Comprehensive Monetary Arrangements: Financial strength is intently attached to social dependability. Comprehensive financial strategies that focus on impartial abundance circulation, work creation, and admittance to open doors add to cultural versatility. States ought to zero in on restricting pay variations and establishing conditions where all residents can take part in and benefit from monetary development.

   Worldwide Financial Collaboration: In an interconnected world, worldwide monetary participation is fundamental for flexibility. Countries can team up on economic accords, monetary guidelines, and venture systems to advance dependability. Cooperative endeavors, like composed financial and money related strategies, can likewise assist with tending to monetary slumps on a world-wide scale.

2. **Natural Maintainability:**

The flexibility of the worldwide framework is unpredictably connected to ecological maintainability. Environmental change, asset consumption, and natural corruption present huge dangers that request aggregate activity to guarantee a supportable future.

Environmentally friendly power Progress: A strong worldwide framework requires a change to sustainable power sources to moderate the effect of environmental change. Countries can put resources into clean energy framework, embrace manageable practices, and team up on innovative work to speed up the shift toward sustainable power.

Preservation and Biodiversity Assurance: Safeguarding biodiversity and rationing regular assets add to natural flexibility. Countries can team up on preservation drives, take on reasonable land-use practices, and work together to address deforestation and territory misfortune. The safeguarding of biological systems improves the planet's capacity to endure natural shocks.

Worldwide Natural Arrangements: Cooperation in global ecological arrangements, like the Paris Understanding, is vital for worldwide flexibility. Countries can focus on decreasing fossil fuel byproducts, setting aggressive focuses for ecological supportability, and sharing prescribed procedures to on the whole address the difficulties presented by environmental change.

3. **Social Union and Comprehensive Administration:**

A versatile worldwide framework depends on friendly union and comprehensive administration structures that engage residents, encourage trust, and advance participation. Cultural soundness is a foundation of versatility, and countries should focus on friendly consideration, value, and the insurance of basic freedoms.

Comprehensive Approaches and Organizations: Comprehensive administration includes making arrangements and establishments that take special care of the necessities of different populaces. This incorporates tending to social disparities, safeguarding minority privileges, and encouraging comprehensive dynamic cycles. Countries can gain from fruitful models of comprehensive administration to fortify their cultural texture.

Interest in Schooling and Medical services: Building flexibility requires interests in training and medical care. Countries ought to focus on available and top notch training, guaranteeing that residents are furnished with the abilities required for the positions representing things to come. Available medical services frameworks contribute not exclusively to individual prosperity yet additionally to the general flexibility of social orders.

Social Wellbeing Nets: Strong social security nets assume an essential part in the midst of emergency. Countries can lay out and fortify social government assistance programs that offer monetary help, medical services, and instruction to weak populaces. These security nets improve the strength of social orders by forestalling the compounding of social disparities during testing times.

4. **Mechanical Advancement and Coordinated effort:**

Mechanical development is a main impetus behind flexibility in the cutting edge time. Embracing mechanical headways and encouraging worldwide coordinated effort in the domain of development add to a strong worldwide framework.

Computerized Change: The advanced change of social orders improves flexibility by giving new devices to correspondence, training, and remote work. Countries can put resources into computerized framework, advance mechanical proficiency, and influence arising innovations, for example, man-made consciousness to improve productivity and versatility.

Worldwide Innovative work Associations: Cooperative innovative work drives reinforce worldwide flexibility. Countries can pool assets and aptitude to address normal difficulties, whether in medical care, environment science, or innovation. Open sharing of logical information speeds up progress and prepares countries to handle arising dangers on the whole.

Network protection Coordinated effort: With the rising digitization of social orders, online protection is principal for versatility. Countries can team up on network safety measures, share danger insight, and lay out global standards to forestall digital dangers. A solid computerized climate is fundamental for monetary steadiness, public safety, and the security of basic framework.

Chapter 9

Looking Ahead

As we stand at the limit representing things to come, looking into the obscure, the scene before us is molded by a juncture of difficulties and open doors that request prescience, versatility, and aggregate activity. Looking forward, we end up exploring a complicated and dynamic worldwide climate, where the decisions today will shape the direction of tomorrow. This investigation dives into the complex parts of looking forward, incorporating innovative headways, international movements, cultural changes, and the basic for maintainable turn of events.

1. **Innovative Outskirts:**
   The speeding up speed of mechanical advancement is a certain power that will characterize the forms representing things to come. As we look forward, a few key mechanical boondocks are ready to reshape the manner in which we live, work, and connect.
   Man-made reasoning and AI: The development of computerized reasoning (simulated intelligence) and AI remains as a groundbreaking power with sweeping ramifications. As calculations become more complex and equipped for independent navigation, ventures going from medical care to fund will go through extremist changes. Moral contemplations encompassing man-made intelligence, including issues of predisposition and responsibility, will request cautious route.
   Quantum Figuring: The approach of quantum registering vows to alter data handling, taking care of mind boggling issues at speeds unbelievable with old style PCs. This has significant ramifications for fields like cryptography, materials science, and improvement issues. As quantum advancements mature, their mix into different areas will open new wildernesses of plausibility.
   Biotechnology and Genomics: Advances in biotechnology and genomics are introducing a period of customized medication, quality altering, and creative answers for squeezing worldwide wellbeing challenges. The crossing point of science and innovation holds the commitment of forward leaps in illness

treatment, rural practices, and natural protection. Be that as it may, moral contemplations encompassing hereditary control and security will request cautious moral and administrative systems.

5G and Network: The boundless execution of 5G innovation will push us into a time of unmatched availability. The Web of Things (IoT) will prosper, empowering consistent correspondence among gadgets and working with the ascent of brilliant urban areas. The ramifications for enterprises, from assembling to medical care, are significant, offering expanded effectiveness and advancement.

2. **International Elements:**

The international scene is in a condition of steady motion, molded by power shifts, territorial elements, and the exchange of worldwide powers. Looking forward, a few key international patterns will impact the overall influence and the idea of global relations.

Ascent of Multipolarity: The development of numerous focuses of force, including China, India, and local coalitions, flags a shift towards a multipolar world. This multipolarity presents the two open doors for coordinated effort and difficulties connected with contest and expected irreconcilable situations. Exploring this multipolar scene will require proficient discretion and vital premonition.

Mechanical Rivalry: International elements are progressively affected by innovative contest, especially in regions like man-made intelligence, digital abilities, and space investigation. Countries are competing for predominance in these basic spaces, as mechanical ability turns into a critical determinant of international impact.

Environment Strategy: The worldwide basic to address environmental change is reshaping political relations. Countries are perceiving the interconnectedness of natural difficulties and the requirement for cooperative arrangements. Environment tact will assume a urgent part in molding peaceful accords, asset distribution, and systems for manageable turn of events.

Network safety Worries: As our reality turns out to be all the more carefully associated, the meaning of online protection in international contemplations develops. Countries are wrestling with the difficulties of guarding against digital dangers, guaranteeing the respectability of basic framework, and exploring the developing scene of digital fighting.

3. **Cultural Changes:**

Cultural changes are unfurling at an uncommon speed, driven by segment shifts, social elements, and developing qualities. Looking forward, these cultural changes will impact how we characterize personality, collaborate with each other, and shape the organizations that oversee our lives.

Segment Movements: Maturing populaces, relocation examples, and changes in rates of birth are reshaping segment scenes. Countries should address the ramifications of these movements on medical services frameworks, work markets, and social government assistance structures. Overseeing variety and encouraging social attachment even with segment changes will be basic.

Redefinition of Work: The idea of work is going through an extreme change, prodded by mechanical progressions and the ascent of remote and adaptable work game plans. The gig economy, mechanization, and the reexamination of balance between fun and serious activities are reshaping customary business models. Legislatures and enterprises should adjust strategies to guarantee the prosperity of laborers and explore the difficulties of a quickly developing position market.

Social Elements: Developing social elements, including evolving standards, perspectives, and social developments, are molding the texture of social orders. Developments for civil rights, orientation fairness, and social inclusivity are picking up speed. Recognizing and embracing assorted viewpoints will be fundamental for cultivating comprehensive social orders that mirror the upsides of correspondence and equity.

Emotional well-being Mindfulness: The acknowledgment of emotional well-being as a basic part of in general prosperity is acquiring conspicuousness. Social orders are turning out to be more sensitive to the significance of psychological well-being mindfulness, destigmatizing psychological well-being issues, and putting resources into emotionally supportive networks. States and foundations should focus on psychological well-being as a basic piece of general wellbeing plans.

4. **Economical Advancement Basic:**

The basic for economical advancement poses a potential threat not too far off as the worldwide local area faces natural difficulties, imbalance, and the requirement for dependable asset the executives. Looking forward, the quest for manageability will shape arrangements, strategic policies, and worldwide participation.

Sustainable power Progress: The desperation to address environmental change is driving a worldwide change to environmentally friendly power sources. Legislatures, organizations, and networks are embracing manageable works on, putting resources into clean energy foundation, and reconsidering energy utilization examples to diminish carbon impressions.

Roundabout Economy: The shift towards a roundabout economy, described by decreasing waste, reusing materials, and reusing, is building up momentum. This approach plans to limit natural effect and make feasible creation and utilization cycles. Embracing roundabout economy standards will be fundamental for relieving asset exhaustion and natural corruption.

Comprehensive Financial Models: Practical improvement requires comprehensive monetary models that focus on fair abundance circulation, neediness decrease, and social prosperity. Countries should reevaluate financial approaches to guarantee that development helps all sections of society, tending to inconsistencies and cultivating strength against monetary shocks.

Worldwide Wellbeing Readiness: The experience of the Coronavirus pandemic has highlighted the significance of worldwide wellbeing readiness. Countries should put resources into powerful medical services frameworks, improve global participation on wellbeing emergencies, and focus on innovative work in the areas of virology and the study of disease transmission.

9.1 Reflection on the Political Evolution

As we leave on an intelligent excursion through the records of political development, the embroidery of mankind's set of experiences unfurls with complicated examples of progress, variation, and outlook changes. The tale of political development is a demonstration of the flexibility, resourcefulness, and intricacy of human social orders as they explore the rhythmic movement of time. This reflection digs into the groundbreaking excursion of political frameworks, investigating key achievements, fundamental powers, and the getting through examples that shape how we might interpret administration, power, and the persistent quest for cultural advancement.

1. **Old Establishments:**

   The starting points of political advancement can be followed to the support of development, where antiquated social orders established the groundworks for administration structures that would reverberate through centuries. From the city-territories of Mesopotamia to the complexities of Egyptian administration, early civilizations wrestled with the basic inquiry of how to sort out and oversee human issues. Governments, theocracies, and the appearance of early vote based systems in Athens denoted the beginning endeavors to classify the connection among rulers and the dominated.

   Examples from Days of yore: The political advancement of old social orders grants persevering through illustrations. The fragile harmony between concentrated power and the privileges of residents, the job of regulation in forming administration, and the seeds of popularity based goals established in the ripe soil of days of yore keep on resounding in contemporary political idea.

2. **Feudalism to Renaissance:**

   The middle age time introduced the predominance of feudalism, a progressive framework where land possession gave power. Nonetheless, the Renaissance went about as an impetus for a seismic shift, with the recovery of old style learning, the coming of humanism, and the scrutinizing of customary power. The Gutenberg print machine turned into a harbinger of mass correspondence, testing the syndication of information held by the elites.

   Development of Country Expresses: The political advancement of the Renaissance laid the foundation for the ascent of country states. Governments solidified power, encouraging a feeling of public personality. The Tranquility of Westphalia in 1648 denoted a significant second, perceiving the sway of individual states and making way for the cutting edge worldwide framework.

Edification Standards: The Illumination period introduced an intense quest for reason, individual freedoms, and delegate administration. Masterminds like John Locke, Montesquieu, and Rousseau significantly affected political idea. Ideas of regular privileges, the common agreement, and detachment of abilities became philosophical support points that supported the development of current political frameworks.

3. **Progressive Breezes:**

The eighteenth and nineteenth hundreds of years saw the breezes of unrest clearing across the globe. The American Upset, the French Transformation, and the Latin American Conflicts of Freedom tested settled in power structures, upholding for standards of freedom, correspondence, and crew. The development of vote based republics denoted a takeoff from monarchical rule.

The Introduction of Current Majority rules government: The political advancement during this period proclaimed the introduction of present day vote based system. The US Constitution, with its arrangement of governing rules, set a trend for delegate administration. The French Upheaval's beliefs of equity under the watchful eye of the law and the freedoms of man resonated worldwide, motivating developments for self-assurance.

Modern Upheaval and Social Developments: The Modern Unrest achieved monetary changes that resonated in the political circle. Social developments arose, supporting for laborers' privileges, ladies' testimonial, and social equality. The developing connection among free enterprise and a vote based system turned into a point of convergence, molding banters about civil rights and the job of the state.

4. **20th 100 years:**

The twentieth century unfurled as a cauldron of political disturbances, worldwide contentions, and philosophical showdowns. The world saw the ascent and fall of extremist systems, the battles for decolonization, and the rise of superpowers secured in a Virus War. The Assembled Countries was laid out to encourage worldwide participation and forestall the repeat of worldwide struggles.

Cold Conflict Elements: The Virus War characterized a large part of the political scene, with the philosophical conflict among socialism and private enterprise forming global relations. The Cuban Rocket Emergency, the weapons contest, and intermediary wars highlighted the trickiness of worldwide strength. The possible breakdown of the Soviet Association denoted the finish of a bipolar world request.

Globalization and Interconnectedness: The last 50% of the twentieth century saw the speed increase of globalization. Monetary relationship, innovative progressions, and the ascent of global foundations changed the idea of political power. Issues, for example, environmental change, basic liberties, and financial disparity became worldwide worries, requiring cooperative arrangements.

5. **Contemporary Scene:**

As we consider the political development into the 21st 100 years, the scene is described by a mind boggling transaction of powers that rise above borders. The quick speed of innovative progressions, the difficulties presented by environmental change, and the complexities of worldwide association characterize the contemporary political landscape.

Advanced Age and Data Transformation: The coming of the computerized age has reclassified the elements of legislative issues. Data streams at remarkable velocities, forming public talk, impacting decisions, and testing customary media scenes. Issues of deception, online security, and the effect of web-based entertainment on political polarization present novel difficulties.

Ascent of Non-State Entertainers: The impact of non-state entertainers, from worldwide companies to non-administrative associations, has developed altogether. These elements employ significant financial and political power, frequently rising above the limits of individual country states. Inquiries of responsibility and administration in this developing scene stay squeezing.

Worldwide Difficulties and Participation: Contemporary political development is set apart by a common acknowledgment of worldwide difficulties that request cooperative arrangements. Environmental change, general well-being emergencies, and the dangers of psychological warfare highlight the need for worldwide collaboration. Multilateral foundations, in spite of difficulties, assume a critical part in exploring these common worries.

6. **Looking Forward:**

As we cast our look forward, the direction of political development seems both promising and laden with difficulties. The basic for responsive administration, comprehensive arrangements, and maintainable improvement has never been more obvious. A few key contemplations will shape the future political scene.

Ecological Stewardship: The earnestness to address natural difficulties, including environmental change and biodiversity misfortune, will be a characterizing part of future political development. Countries should team up on aggressive targets, maintainable practices, and green advances to guarantee the prosperity of the planet.

Innovation and Morals: The moral components of mechanical progressions will be a focal concentration. As man-made reasoning, biotechnology, and computerized developments keep on propelling, inquiries of security, value, and the moral utilization of innovation will shape political talk.

Comprehensive Administration: The call for comprehensive administration that focuses on the freedoms and prosperity, everything being equal, will reverberate. Resolving issues of social disparity, fundamental separation, and the security of common freedoms will be basic for encouraging tough social orders.

Worldwide Collaboration: The requirement for reinforced worldwide participation notwithstanding worldwide difficulties stays principal. Whether tending to general wellbeing emergencies, financial incongruities, or international strains, cooperative tact and multilateralism will be fundamental for a stable worldwide request.

Flexibility Notwithstanding Vulnerability: The future political scene will without a doubt be set apart by vulnerabilities. From the effect of unexpected worldwide occasions to the difficulties presented by fast mechanical progressions, political frameworks should exhibit flexibility and versatility despite developing conditions.

9.2 Lessons Learned and Future Predictions

As we think about the unpredictable embroidered artwork of political development, the illustrations gained from history give significant bits of knowledge into the elements of administration, cultural advancement, and the transaction of force. These examples act as guideposts for exploring the intricacies of the present and expecting the difficulties and valuable open doors that lie ahead. This investigation dives into the key examples gathered from political development and offers reflections on future forecasts, perceiving that the way ahead is formed by the aggregate insight of the past.

1. **The Basic of Comprehensive Administration:**
   A foundation illustration from political development is the basic of comprehensive administration. History gives testimony regarding the results of exclusionary frameworks, where power packed in the possession of a couple of prompted cultural distress and shakiness. From old majority rules systems to current agent republics, the example is clear: administration should be comprehensive, receptive to the necessities, everything being equal, and defensive of their freedoms.
   Reflection on Past Treacheries: Thinking back, snapshots of political disturbance and social developments highlight the getting through battle for inclusivity. Social equality developments, ladies' testimonial, and battles against separation have reliably tested exclusionary standards. These authentic battles stress that progress is unyieldingly connected to the extension of inclusivity in administration.
   Future Forecast - Embracing Variety: The direction of political development focuses towards a future where variety and inclusivity become focal fundamentals of administration. As social orders wrestle with issues of fundamental segregation and social disparity, the call for portrayal, value, and equity will shape political plans. Foreseeing a future where pioneers focus on variety and inclusivity is a consistent expansion of the illustrations gained from verifiable battles.

2. **The Unique Overall influence:**
   A repetitive subject in political development is the unique idea of the overall influence. Whether in the ascent and fall of realms, the rise of country states, or the elements of global relations, the dispersion of force shapes the course of history. Illustrations from the past highlight the significance of governing rules, forestalling the grouping of force that can prompt oppression.

Examples from Governments and Tyrant Rule: The overabundances of out-right governments and dictator systems stand as wake up calls. The maltreatments of force, concealment of dispute, and absence of responsibility feature the perils inborn in uncontrolled power. The illustrations learned advocate for structures that convey power, guaranteeing responsibility and defending against manhandles.

Future Expectation - Advancing Power Elements: Expecting the future, the advancement of force elements will probably proceed. The ascent of local powers, the impact of non-state entertainers, and changes in international scenes recommend a liquid and consistently changing overall influence. Future administration models should explore these intricacies, taking on adaptable and responsive designs.

3. **The Convergence of Innovation and Administration:**
The connection among innovation and administration is an illustration that reverberations through the ages. From the print machine to the computerized age, innovative headways reshape the political scene. The examples learned underline the extraordinary effect of data dispersal, correspondence, and the requirement for moral contemplations in taking on new advancements.

Gutenberg Print machine: The approach of the print machine reformed the spread of data, testing laid out progressive systems and adding to the democratization of information. The examples from this verifiable crossroads highlight the significant effect innovation can have on political designs and public talk.

Future Expectation - Moral Tech Administration: Looking forward, the combination of arising innovations like computerized reasoning, blockchain, and biotechnology into administration will characterize the future political scene. Moral contemplations, security assurances, and capable administration of mechanical headways will be basic in relieving chances and expanding cultural advantages.

4. **Worldwide Interconnectedness and Coordinated effort:**
The examples drawn from political advancement accentuate the rising interconnectedness of the world. Whether through exchange, discretion, or shared difficulties like environmental change, the requirement for worldwide cooperation is a repetitive topic. Countries are complicatedly connected, and the answers for some contemporary issues require helpful endeavors.

Verifiable Partnerships and Joint efforts: Over the entire course of time, unions, deals, and worldwide joint efforts have formed international results. From the Show of Europe to the Class of Countries and the Unified Countries, endeavors at encouraging worldwide collaboration highlight the comprehension that difficulties rise above public lines.

Future Expectation - Transnational Difficulties: Foreseeing what's to come includes perceiving the escalation of transnational difficulties. Issues like environmental change, pandemics, and online protection dangers require worldwide participation. Future administration models will probably underline the significance of cooperative structures, with worldwide associations assuming a urgent part in tending to shared difficulties.

5. **The Job of Common Society and Grassroots Developments:**
The examples from political advancement feature the catalyzing job of common society and grassroots developments. Social change frequently exudes from the beginning, as standard residents prepare for equity, uniformity, and the security of privileges. Whether in the abolitionist developments, work strikes, or contemporary civil rights dissents, the effect of grassroots developments is significant.
Tradition of Social Developments: The abrogation of subjection, the suffragette developments, and the social equality time embody the groundbreaking force of grassroots developments. These verifiable battles accentuate the organization of people and networks in molding political results.
Future Forecast - Enabled Common Society: The direction of political development recommends a future where common society assumes an undeniably engaged part. Virtual entertainment and advanced stages intensify the voices of people, empowering mass assembly and backing. Future administration models should draw in with and answer the worries and goals of a functioning and informed common society.

6. **Flexibility Even with Change:**

Maybe one of the most persevering through illustrations from political development is the requirement for flexibility despite change. Social orders that endured changes, emergencies, and groundbreaking minutes were those that exhibited flexibility and an ability to adjust their political frameworks to new real factors.

Examples from Fundamental Changes: The fall of domains, the finish of pilgrim rule, and the breakdown of philosophical systems epitomize the versatility basic. Political frameworks that opposed change frequently confronted interior conflict or outer tensions, featuring the certainty of transformation even with cultural, financial, and international movements.

Future Forecast - Responsive Administration: Anticipating what's in store highlights the significance of responsive administration. Social orders will probably confront exceptional difficulties, from the effects of mechanization on work to the moral predicaments presented by biotechnology. Administration models that can adjust, improve, and answer these difficulties will be significant for guaranteeing dependability and progress.

9.3 The Role of Citizens in Shaping the Future

In the unpredictable embroidery of administration, the job of residents arises as a key part, a powerful power that winds around together the texture of cultural advancement and political development.

Residents, on the whole comprising the heartbeat of a country, assume a crucial part in forming the direction representing things to come. This investigation dives into the diverse elements of the populace's job, enveloping urban commitment, social obligation, and the strengthening of people in impacting the shapes of administration.

1. **Community Commitment as the Foundation:**
   At the core of the resident's job in forming what's in store lies the idea of community commitment. Urban commitment envelops a range of exercises through which people take part in the existence of their networks, voice their interests, and effectively add to the dynamic cycles that oversee their lives. It rises above the demonstration of casting a ballot and reaches out into different types of support, local area administration, and informed talk.

   Casting a ballot as an Essential Right: The foundation of urban commitment is the key right to cast a ballot. Decisions act as a foundation of vote based social orders, offering residents the ability to pick their delegates and shape the bearing of administration. In practicing their democratic freedoms, residents add to the majority rule process, affecting the arrangement of assemblies and chief bodies.

   Past the Polling station: Be that as it may, urban commitment reaches out past the demonstration of projecting voting forms. Dynamic cooperation in local area drives, grassroots developments, and common society associations enhances the aggregate voice of residents. By going to municipal events, taking part out in the open discussions, and partaking in backing efforts, people add to the dynamic quality of popularity based talk.

2. **The Elements of Social Obligation:**
   Vital to the resident's job is the idea of social obligation, a moral and moral basic to add to the prosperity of the bigger local area. Social obligation reaches out past individual interests, underscoring a guarantee to the benefit of everyone and the headway of cultural objectives.

   Local area Building and Strengthening: Residents, as dynamic members in the social texture, add to local area building and strengthening. Chipping in for neighborhood drives, supporting instructive projects, and cultivating a feeling of having a place reinforce the social bonds that support steady and strong social orders.

   Ecological Stewardship: An essential part of social obligation in the contemporary period is natural stewardship. Residents bear an aggregate liability regarding the manageable utilization of assets, the relief of environmental change, and the protection of biodiversity. Drives going from squander decrease to maintainable way of life decisions exhibit the resident's job in advancing an agreeable relationship with the climate.

3. **Enabling People to Drive Change:**
   The resident's job in molding what's to come stretches out past detached support; it includes enabling people to be dynamic problem solvers. Strengthening

suggests furnishing residents with the instruments, information, and office to straightforwardly impact the choices that influence their lives.

Admittance to Data: Data is an incredible asset for strengthening. In the advanced age, residents have uncommon admittance to data that permits them to remain informed about government activities, cultural issues, and worldwide patterns. A very much educated populace is better prepared to connect seriously in just cycles and consider people with great influence responsible.

Support and Activism: Strengthening is manifest in promotion and activism. People who feel engaged perceive their capacity to impact change. Whether pushing for strategy changes, civil rights, or basic liberties, engaged residents add to a more responsive and comprehensive administration.

4. **Innovation as an Empowering agent of Resident Support:**

   In the contemporary scene, innovation arises as a groundbreaking power, enhancing the resident's voice and cultivating new roads for support. The approach of advanced stages, virtual entertainment, and online activism has re-classified the elements of resident commitment.

   Advanced Majority rules government: Innovation works with computerized vote based system, giving residents stages to communicate their perspectives, activate support, and take part in aggregate activity. Web-based entertainment stages act as virtual town squares, where conversations on approach issues, activism, and mindfulness crusades thrive.

   E-Administration and Community Tech: States, as well, influence innovation to upgrade resident commitment. E-administration drives and urban tech stages smooth out admittance to public administrations, empower online conferences, and work with direct correspondence among residents and leaders. The joining of innovation cultivates a more responsive and straightforward administration system.

5. **The Critical Job of Instruction:**

   Instruction arises as an impetus for viable resident support. Informed residents, furnished with decisive reasoning abilities and a profound comprehension of cultural issues, are more ready to take part in significant discourse, settle on informed decisions, and add to the popularity based process.

   Municipal Training: Integrating metro schooling into educational plans enables understudies to grasp the standards of a majority rules system, the working of government, and their freedoms as well as limitations as residents. City schooling lays the basis for an educated and drew in populace since the beginning.

   Long lasting Learning: Training isn't restricted to formal tutoring; it is a deep rooted pursuit. Empowering constant finding out about administration structures, worldwide issues, and cultural difficulties guarantees that residents stay educated and versatile in a steadily developing world.

6. **The Call for Inclusivity and Variety:**

In forming the future, the resident's job requires a promise to inclusivity and the festival of variety. Perceiving the lavishness of assorted viewpoints, encounters, and foundations improves the vote based process and guarantees that administration is intelligent of the pluralistic idea of social orders.

Comprehensive Exchange: Residents add to molding the future through comprehensive discourse. Embracing assorted voices, participating in discussions that envelop a range of conclusions, and encouraging a climate where alternate points of view are esteemed improve the political talk and lead to more comprehensive navigation.

Backing for Equivalent Portrayal: The resident's job remembers upholding for equivalent portrayal for administration structures. This includes testing foundational hindrances that limit the support of minimized gatherings and pushing for arrangements that advance variety in political administration.

www.ingramcontent.com/pod-product-compliance
Lightning Source LLC
LaVergne TN
LVHW051304200726
843510LV00010B/1271